THE CAMBRIDGE BIBLE COMMENTARY

NEW ENGLISH BIBLE

GENERAL EDITORS
P. R. ACKROYD, A. R. C. LEANEY, J. W. PACKER

THE LETTERS OF PAUL
TO THE PHILIPPIANS
AND TO THE
THESSALONIANS

THE CAMBRIDGE BIBLE COMMENTARY

THE LETTERS OF PAUL
TO THE PHILIPPIANS
AND TO THE
THESSALONIANS

COMMENTARY BY

KENNETH GRAYSTON
Professor of Theology, University of Bristol

CAMBRIDGE
AT THE UNIVERSITY PRESS
1967

Published by the Syndics of the Cambridge University Press
Bentley House, 200 Euston Road, London, N.W. 1
American Branch: 32 East 57th Street, New York, N.Y. 10022

© Cambridge University Press 1967

Library of Congress Catalogue Card Number: 67–18312

Printed in Great Britain
at the University Printing House, Cambridge
(Brooke Crutchley, University Printer)

GENERAL EDITORS' PREFACE

The aim of this series is to provide the text of the New English Bible closely linked to a commentary in which the results of modern scholarship are made available to the general reader. Teachers and young people preparing for such examinations as the General Certificate of Education at Ordinary or Advanced Level in Britain, and for similar qualifications elsewhere, have been especially kept in mind. The commentators have been asked to assume no specialized theological knowledge, and no knowledge of Greek and Hebrew. Bare references to other literature and multiple references to other parts of the Bible have been avoided. Actual quotations have been given as often as possible.

Within these quite severe limits each commentator will attempt to set out the main findings of recent New Testament scholarship, and to describe the historical background to the text. The main theological content of the New Testament will also be critically discussed.

Much attention has been given to the form of the volumes. The aim is to produce books each of which will be read consecutively from first to last page. The introductory material leads naturally into the text, which itself leads into the alternating sections of commentary.

The series is prefaced by a volume—*Understanding the New Testament*—which outlines the larger historical background, says something about the growth and transmission of the text, and answers the question 'Why should we study the New Testament?' Another volume—*New Testament Illustrations*—contains maps, diagrams and photographs.　　　　P. R. A.　　A. R. C. L.　　J. W. P.

CONTENTS

CONTENTS

THE LETTER OF PAUL
TO THE PHILIPPIANS

THE LETTER OF PAUL TO
THE PHILIPPIANS

✳ ✳ ✳ ✳ ✳ ✳ ✳ ✳ ✳ ✳ ✳ ✳ ✳

THE LETTER OR LETTERS

Philippians hangs together rather less successfully than most
of Paul's letters. There is no problem about the early part
(1: 1 — 3: 1), which begins with the familiar thanksgiving
and prayer, describes Paul's situation, appeals for unity and
obedience, discloses plans to send Timothy and Epaphroditus
to Philippi, and seems to be coming to an end with suitable
farewell messages. But at this point there is a remarkable inter-
ruption: with scarcely any warning, Paul launches into a
vigorous attack on opponents, one thing leads to another, and
the original mood is not resumed until 4: 2 at the earliest. Here
are the farewell messages (4: 2–9) and the letter seems to be
coming to an end. But then it starts up afresh, with a long and
elaborate thanksgiving for a gift which the Philippians had
sent to Paul by Epaphroditus (4: 10–20). And at last there is a
real closing paragraph (4: 21–3).

There may have been perfectly good reasons for this lack of
coherence, but many scholars are persuaded that the present
Letter to the Philippians contains as many as three Pauline
letters (or part-letters) joined together in somewhat dis-
ordered fashion. Several plausible re-arrangements are possible.
There is a letter of gratitude, contained in 4: 10–20, for the
gift of the Philippian church when Paul was in some kind of
trouble, and conveyed by one of their number called Epaphroditus. This letter was sent soon after the delivery of the gift.

In a second letter, contained perhaps in 1: 1 — 3: 1 and
4: 2–9 (perhaps also 4: 21–3, though these verses could be the
ending of any of the letters), Paul tells them how things have

3

gone with him since he last wrote. He is in prison and expecting to be tried on a charge that may mean death. His
companion is Timothy, whom he proposes to send to Philippi
on a visit of inspection, as soon as his affair has been settled.
Epaphroditus has been seriously ill and is therefore sent back to
Philippi as bearer of the letter. Other news is given of the
situation of the church in the city where Paul is imprisoned,
and there is an appeal for unity and harmony among the
Christians of Philippi.

The remainder, 3: 2 — 4: 1 (unless 4: 2–9 should be included here), is part of a third letter attacking dangerous opponents and countering their views with Paul's own principles of
renunciation and striving for perfection. Perhaps this letter
was sent after the other two, but it contains no indication of
Paul's situation or of the position at Philippi. Indeed, the
readers are not identified though it seems that they have had
previous letters from Paul.

This division of the letter is persuasive, as far as it goes; but
it is difficult to see why someone at an early time should have
combined three letters in this strange order. It would be worth
while taking the division seriously if it solved some problems
of the letter that cannot otherwise be understood. It can scarcely
be said that it solves any problems of interpretation: since the
letter is in any case rather disjointed, each main section has
to be interpreted on its own whether it is three letters or one.
On the other hand it may contribute something to the
question about where the letter was written.

AN OUTLINE OF THE LETTER

4

PAUL'S IMPRISONMENT

Paul is in prison, expecting a trial which may result in his
execution, but more probably an acquittal—in which case he
will visit Philippi again. This is made clear by such remarks as
the following: 'when I lie in prison or appear in the dock'
(1: 7), 'the issue of it all will be my deliverance' (1: 19),
'whether through my life or through my death' (1: 20), and
'when I am with you again' (1: 26).

There are three other New Testament letters written by
Paul from prison—Ephesians, Colossians, and Philemon—
which are closely related in ideas, wording and people mentioned. Apart from the mention of Timothy in the opening
verses of Colossians and Philippians, there are no such links
between Philippians and the other three.

Where could Paul have been imprisoned? Acts mentions
only three imprisonments: at Philippi (16: 23–40) when the
gospel was first preached there; at Caesarea (23: 35 — 26: 32)

for two years awaiting trial on Jewish charges; and at Rome
(28: 16–31) after his appeal to Caesar. But in 2 Cor. 11: 23,
which must have been written before the imprisonment at
Caesarea, Paul says that he was 'more often imprisoned' than
his rivals. Therefore Acts probably omits some occasions of
imprisonment.

The references in Phil. 1: 13 to 'headquarters' (in Greek,
praetorium) and in 4: 22 to the 'imperial establishment'
(R.S.V., 'Caesar's household') would suit an imprisonment
in the provinces as well as in Rome. But if we rightly interpret passages in the letter to mean that Paul was facing the
possibility of judicial execution, then Rome was the place of
his imprisonment. From anywhere else, as a Roman citizen
he could appeal to Caesar. What the letter discloses of Paul's
relations with his companions and the local Christians suits
the statement of Acts 28: 30–1 that 'he stayed there two
full years at his own expense, with a welcome for all who
came to him, proclaiming the kingdom of God and teaching
the facts about the Lord Jesus Christ quite openly and without
hindrance'.

But a number of objections have been offered to this
traditional view. For one thing, Paul and the Philippians were
in frequent communication. Presumably news of his imprisonment had reached Philippi, the Philippians had collected money
and sent it by Epaphroditus, who had been seriously ill
(though we do not know when or where), and a report of
this illness had gone to Philippi. It is possible (though perhaps
not likely) that someone had brought back the information
that the Philippians were worried about Epaphroditus. That
required at least three journeys to or from Philippi since Paul
was imprisoned; and there were more to come. Timothy was
to visit the church and report back, by which time Paul
hoped to be free to visit them himself. Now the journey from
Rome to Philippi was complicated—360 miles by road from
Rome to Brundisium, then by ship to Dyrrachium, requiring
one or two days, and another 380 miles along the Via Egnatia

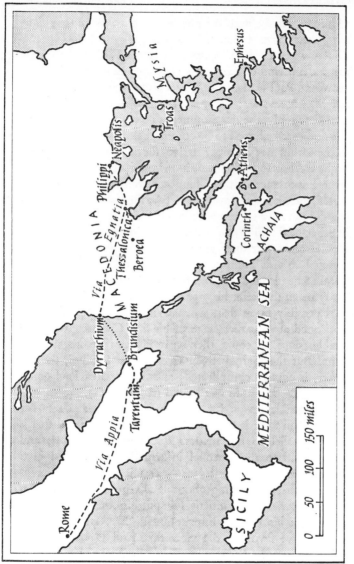

PAUL AND PHILIPPI

to Philippi. At the standard rate of travel of 15 miles a day, each journey would require 50 days.

There was, of course, plenty of time for all this journeying during the period of two years at Rome mentioned in Acts. But would Paul wait so long to acknowledge the Philippians' gift? (If, however, 4: 10–20 is a separate letter containing his immediate reply, the question needs no answer.) Would Paul have said that he hoped to be coming before long (2: 24) if in fact he could not possibly arrive for at least six months? Ought we not to look for an imprisonment nearer Philippi?

The importance of these supposed journeys can be exaggerated, since it is quite possible to take the view that Epaphroditus did not have to wait for news before setting out with the gift; that he fell ill in the course of his journey, and was sent home at once. But there are other objections to Rome. Paul proposed to visit Philippi again, but according to Rom. 15: 24 and 28 he planned to go on from Rome to Spain. This may simply mean that after his arrest the situation changed, but it could possibly mean that, when writing Philippians, he was imprisoned at an earlier stage of his life. Caesarea would be possible, since he could then visit Philippi on his way to Rome. But the journey from Caesarea to Philippi, though shorter, is equally complicated; and at Caesarea Paul could appeal to Caesar—as in fact he did (Acts 25: 11).

One possible reason for putting Philippians at an earlier stage in Paul's life is that chapter 3 contains material that is closely parallel to the matters discussed in Galatians and Romans and to the personal information mentioned in 2 Corinthians. Of course, if 3: 2 — 4: 1 is part of a different letter which says nothing about Paul's imprisonment, then this cannot be an argument for putting the whole letter earlier than his Roman imprisonment. Nevertheless, many scholars have favoured the view that Paul was imprisoned during his stay in Ephesus recorded in Acts 19: 1 — 20: 1, around which period the Galatian, Corinthian and Roman letters most probably were written.

8

It is not impossible that Paul was imprisoned as a result of the serious disturbance caused by the Ephesian silversmiths, though Acts 19: 23–41 does not say so. Paul indeed says that he 'fought wild beasts at Ephesus' (1 Cor. 15: 32) and compares himself to 'men condemned to death in the arena' (1 Cor. 4: 9). These remarks are usually thought to be metaphors, but it is possible that they ought to be taken literally.

It would be irregular but not impossible for a Roman citizen to be treated in this way. In 2 Cor. 1: 8–9, Paul speaks of being in such severe trouble in the province of Asia that 'we felt in our hearts that we had received a death-sentence'. But it is not very probable that this refers to an imprisonment at Ephesus. Why should Acts suppress so serious a matter, especially as Paul's discharge would have been a point in his favour? If Paul had really been exposed in the arena, why does he not mention it in his catalogue of troubles in 2 Cor. 11: 23–7? An imprisonment at Ephesus would make the journeys to Philippi much easier, but the evidence for it is lacking, and the probabilities are against it.

The only result of this investigation is that we cannot be quite certain where and when the letter was written. The view that divides the letter into three undermines some of the objections to Rome, and on other grounds Rome is still the most likely place for the writing of Philippians. This uncertainty is a nuisance to anyone who wishes to place the Pauline letters in their order of writing (to discover, for instance, whether there are changes in Paul's thought in the course of his life); but it scarcely matters when interpreting the letter by itself.

PAUL AND THE PHILIPPIAN CHURCH

According to the account in Acts, Paul was hindered from continuing his missionary activity in the province of Asia and was persuaded by a vision to cross into the province of Macedonia and try again there. He went by ship 'to Neapolis, and from there to Philippi, a city of the first rank in that district of Macedonia, and a Roman colony' (Acts 16: 11–12). Philippi enjoyed this special position because it had been settled with soldiers disbanded from the Roman army (in the years 42 and 30 B.C.) who had been granted the same rights as if their land were part of Italy itself.

Naturally the citizens were provided with priests and altars for carrying on the official worship of the Roman state, and they also had a very wide choice of Roman, Greek and foreign gods. At the time of Paul's arrival, the city of Philippi fully shared the hospitality of the age towards many forms of worship and its readiness to combine several cults into one.

Paul's first approach was made to the small Jewish community, and his earliest converts were Lydia, a business woman from the province of Asia and her staff of servants and assistants; then by chance a Greek slave-girl who was a fortune-teller, and a minor government official in charge of the local prison (Acts 16: 14–34). The writer of Acts tells a lively and impressive story about these last two converts, and about Paul's imprisonment, but there is no further information about the church. Not long afterwards Paul referred to 'all the injury and outrage which... we had suffered at Philippi' when he wrote to the Thessalonians (1 Thess. 2: 2).

Despite this difficult beginning, a devoted group of Christians was formed and they twice sent him support when he was in Thessalonica (Phil. 4: 16). No doubt they later joined in the support given by the Macedonian churches (2 Cor. 11: 9) to Paul in Corinth and in their contribution to the common fund for relief of the Jerusalem Christians (2 Cor. 8: 1–2). During Paul's long stay at Ephesus, he sent Timothy to visit the Macedonian churches (Acts 19: 22), and then himself visited the region on his way from Ephesus to Corinth (Acts 20: 1–2, with probably another reference to the same visit in 2 Cor. 2: 13 and 7: 5–6). From Corinth he went north again and spent the Passover season at Philippi before beginning his final journey to Jerusalem (Acts 20: 6).

From the letter itself we can learn a little more. The Christians at Philippi have their opponents and not only believe in Christ but also suffer for him (1: 28–9). They must beware of dangerous enemies of the Christian faith (3: 2–3 and 3: 18); but they must equally be on their guard against internal rivalry and dissension. There is a hint that Paul expects some disagreement with his views (3: 15); but throughout the letter he gives evidence of deep affection for this group of Christians. In no other letter does he share his inner spiritual life so freely with his readers.

* * * * * * * * * * * * *

The Apostle and his Friends

GREETING

FROM PAUL and Timothy, servants of Christ Jesus, to 1 all those of God's people, incorporate in Christ Jesus, who live at Philippi, including their bishops and deacons.

Grace to you and peace from God our Father and the 2 Lord Jesus Christ.

* The standard beginning of an ancient letter is here filled out with special Christian language. *Paul and Timothy* (Timothy appears again at 2: 19–24) describe themselves as Christ's *servants*, using the same word that is translated 'slave' when applied to Christ at 2: 7. Such self-description would have sounded somewhat repugnant to a Greek, unless he was familiar with the Greek Old Testament where the word is commonly used to express the relation of Israelites, especially Moses and the prophets, to the Lord God. In ordinary Greek life a slave was obedient to his lord and wholly at his service; in Jewish religion the slave had the high privilege of being one through whom the Lord did his work and achieved his will. Thus *servants of Christ Jesus* indicates Paul's conception of his own work as well as Christ's significance to him, which is made quite explicit when he joins *the Lord Jesus Christ* with *God our Father*.

The Christians at Philippi are *God's people, incorporate in Christ Jesus*. The conventional translation (as in R.S.V.) is 'saints in Christ Jesus'. There the first word is another borrowing from the Greek Old Testament where it is a very common description of the holy people of God, i.e. the Israelites marked out as obedient to God and devoted to his service. The phrase *in Christ Jesus* and its equivalent 'in the Lord' are fundamental building units, as it were, in the construction of Paul's thought, and they serve many purposes. In this letter, when the phrase is used about God's activity, the translation is simply 'in Christ Jesus', e.g. 'God's call to the life above, in Christ Jesus' at 3: 14, and similarly 4: 7, 19. But when, as here, it describes the communion of believers with Christ and with one another, a paraphrase is needed to bring out its full implications. Hence the use of the unusual word *incorporate* here and at 3: 9, and of the semi-technical word 'fellowship' at 2: 29 and 4: 21. A simpler solution was possible at 2: 1, where 'our common life in Christ' gives the sense.

Who the *bishops and deacons* were, and why Paul specially mentions them, is not known. 'Bishop' conventionally represents the Greek *episkopos* which means a person who exercises almost any kind of supervision. The groups attached to the Qumran community included persons given the name *mebakker* which also means supervisor. They seem to have had responsibility for admitting new members and teaching them the community rule, caring for all members, and acting as the final arbiter of orthodoxy and right conduct. (The many problems about the Qumran leadership are well discussed by G. Vermes, *The Dead Sea Scrolls in English*, pages 18–25.) But it is obviously unlikely that a mainly Gentile church in Macedonia would have modelled its organization on a closed sect of Jews in Palestine. Elsewhere, *episkopoi* are not mentioned by Paul outside the Pastoral letters (e.g. 1 Tim. 3:2; Titus 1: 7); nor does he refer to church leaders except in the most general terms, e.g. 'those who are working so hard among you and in the Lord's fellowship are your leaders and counsellors' (1 Thess. 5: 12). Even when *episkopoi* are mentioned, they seem to be the same persons as 'elders' in a neighbouring passage (cf. the 'elders' in Titus 1: 5 with the 'bishop' in 1: 7; in 1 Tim. 3:2 N.E.B. translates *episkopos* by 'leader...or bishop'). It may be that the *episkopoi* at Philippi had some special responsibility for the gift which had been sent to Paul, since in Greek life a person with financial duties could sometimes be called by this name.

Deacon conventionally represents the Greek *diakonos* and means a person who performs any kind of service. Outside Rom. 16: 1 and the Pastoral Letters it does not appear as an official title, but Paul often applies it to himself and to other Christian missionaries. All that can be learnt from this passing reference is that the Church included a group of leaders and helpers—which is scarcely surprising. ✻

THANKSGIVING AND PRAYER

I thank my God whenever I think of you; and when I pray for you all, my prayers are always joyful, because of the part you have taken in the work of the Gospel from the first day until now. Of one thing I am certain: the One who started the good work in you will bring it to completion by the Day of Christ Jesus. It is indeed only right that I should feel like this about you all, because you hold me in such affection, and because, when I lie in prison or appear in the dock to vouch for the truth of the Gospel, you all share in the privilege that is mine. God knows how I long for you all, with the deep yearning of Christ Jesus himself. And this is my prayer, that your 3, 4 5 6 7 8 9

love may grow ever richer and richer in knowledge and
10 insight of every kind, and may thus bring you the gift of
true discrimination. Then on the Day of Christ you will
11 be flawless and without blame, reaping the full harvest of
righteousness that comes through Jesus Christ, to the
glory and praise of God.

* According to Paul's custom, the first main section is a
thanksgiving for the readers of his letter, and a prayer for
their well-being. He goes beyond mere convention by intro-
ducing at once a note of deep feeling, especially in the word
joyful which announces one of the dominant themes of this
letter. This joy is expressed exclusively in relation to the
Christians at Philippi—as he prays for them, begs them to
think and feel alike (2: 2), contemplates his self-offering for
them (2: 17), tells them to stand firm (4: 1), and remembers
their gift to him (4:10). Correspondingly he expects their
joy to match his, as he bids them rejoice (2: 18; 3: 1; 4: 4)
and encourages them to look forward to his and Timothy's
return (1: 25; 2: 28).

5. *The part you have taken* may refer generally to their own
activity in spreading the gospel, or more particularly to their
help in the early days of Paul's mission and their recent gift
(4: 10, 15, 16).

6. The earliest Christian expectation that *the Day of Christ
Jesus* would soon come, when God would complete what he
had begun and Christians would receive the reward of their
obedience (verses 10–11), still plays an important part in
Paul's language of prayer. As in the earlier Thessalonian
letters, these terms still express the final purpose of his own
life, for at the Day of Christ he expects to offer proof that he
did not 'work in vain' (2: 16). He hopes that he may 'finally
arrive at the resurrection from the dead' (3: 11) when the
Lord Jesus Christ comes as deliverer from heaven and trans-
figures 'the body belonging to our humble state' (3: 20–1).

But in the Thessalonian letters *the Day of Christ Jesus* comes first in his thoughts and he takes it for granted that he will be alive when Christ returns (1 Thess. 4: 15 'we who are left alive until the Lord comes'). In Philippians, however, he is thinking very much about his own death or survival, and has come to realize that he may die before Christ's return.

7. It is not easy to be sure of the exact meaning of this verse. The Greek is in part ambiguous and, instead of *It is indeed only right...*, could be translated: 'I am justified in taking this view about you all, because I hold you in closest union, as those who, when I lie in prison or appear in the dock to vouch for the truth of the Gospel, all share in the privilege that is mine.' The words *appear in the dock* represent the Greek word *apologia*, which can indeed mean a defence in court, but could also be understood in the more general sense it has in 1: 16 ('to defend the Gospel'). And finally, the word *privilege* represents the Greek word translated 'grace' in the greeting and the close of the letter (1: 2 and 4: 23). In many Pauline letters, though not in Thessalonians and Philippians, 'grace' plays an important part in the theological argument. It means God's generous love to unworthy and thankless people shown in Christ's self-sacrifice for them. By the same grace they are called to be God's people and to serve him 'in the work of the Gospel'. Paul regards it as a special grace or privilege that he should be allowed *to vouch for the truth of the Gospel* by imprisonment and trial.

9. *Knowledge* refers to the new awareness of God available to those who have become Christians; *insight* to their ability to make moral decisions.

10. The opening words of this verse can almost be called a Greek cliché, and translation makes the phrase sound more precise than it is. Instead of *may thus bring you the gift of true discrimination*, the N.E.B. footnote offers 'may teach you by experience what things are most worth while'. Paul also uses the phrase in Rom. 2: 18 where it is translated 'aware of moral distinctions'.

11. *Reaping the full harvest of righteousness* is an Old Testament tag, e.g. 'Sow for yourselves righteousness, reap the fruit of steadfast love' (Hos. 10: 12 R.S.V.), and introduces the word *righteousness* which has greater significance later on (3: 6, 9). ✻

PAUL'S SITUATION

12 Friends, I want you to understand that the work of the Gospel has been helped on, rather than hindered, by this
13 business of mine. My imprisonment in Christ's cause has become common knowledge to all at headquarters here,
14 and indeed among the public at large; and it has given confidence to most of our fellow-Christians to speak the word of God fearlessly and with extraordinary courage.

15 Some, indeed, proclaim Christ in a jealous and quarrel-
16 some spirit; others proclaim him in true goodwill, and these are moved by love for me; they know that it is to
17 defend the Gospel that I am where I am. But the others, moved by personal rivalry, present Christ from mixed motives, meaning to stir up fresh trouble for me as I lie
18 in prison. What does it matter? One way or another, in pretence or in sincerity, Christ is set forth, and for that I rejoice.

19 Yes, and rejoice I will, knowing well that the issue of it all will be my deliverance, because you are praying for me and the Spirit of Jesus Christ is given me for support.
20 For, as I passionately hope, I shall have no cause to be ashamed, but shall speak so boldly that now as always the greatness of Christ will shine out clearly in my person,
21 whether through my life or through my death. For to me
22 life is Christ, and death gain; but what if my living on in the body may serve some good purpose? Which then

am I to choose? I cannot tell. I am torn two ways: what 23
I should like is to depart and be with Christ; that is better
by far; but for your sake there is greater need for me to 24
stay on in the body. This indeed I know for certain: I 25
shall stay, and stand by you all to help you forward and
to add joy to your faith, so that when I am with you 26
again, your pride in me may be unbounded in Christ
Jesus.

* Paul now gives his readers news about his present situation
(verses 12–18) and then reflects on his hopes and expectations
(verses 19–26). His imprisonment has not depressed the local
Christians but has stirred them to new efforts, though he cannot approve all they are doing. He welcomes those who say,
in effect, 'Since the apostle is imprisoned it is we who must
speak the word of God'; but there are others who seem to write
him off too easily and wish to take charge of the Christian
mission. Paul does not think it is yet time to give up his
apostolic authority, and still intends to control the work he has
begun. Hence his rather savage remark, 'they are all bent on
their own ends, not on the cause of Christ Jesus', when he
admits (2: 20–21) that only Timothy can be entrusted with a
pastoral visit to Philippi. But at this point he sets his readers a
good example (for they too are upset by 'rivalry and personal vanity', 2: 3) by treating his rivals with cheerful toleration.
In a highly personal manner, he then contemplates the
possible outcome if his case comes to trial. He might be ac-
quitted or put to death. According to Acts 24: 5, the Jewish
charge against Paul before the Roman authorities in Palestine
was, 'We have found this man to be a perfect pest, a fomenter
of discord among the Jews all over the world, a ring-leader
of the sect of the Nazarenes'. The charge was political,
though the evidence was mainly religious. If it could be proved
that Paul was the ringleader in causing civil disturbance, then
he was in serious danger; though he himself consistently argued

that the dispute was really about religion. He now thinks that *all at headquarters* have come to realize that his imprisonment is *in Christ's cause*; he is in trouble because of religious convictions (verse 13). This gives him sufficient confidence to think that his release is really possible—at least, just as possible as his death. Not without emotion, he comes to terms with both possibilities.

13. The words *headquarters here* leave the place of Paul's imprisonment an open question. What he actually wrote was *praetorium*, which originally meant the general's tent (or his staff), and came to be used for the Roman governor's residence in the provinces—'the Residency', in the language of British Colonial days. It is used in this way of Pilate's headquarters in Jerusalem (Mark 15: 16). When the governor was at Caesarea, he used Herod's palace as his headquarters and Paul was imprisoned there (Acts 23: 35). In Rome itself this name would not have been used for the imperial palace (though a provincial like Paul may so have used it), and Praetorium there would mean the imperial guard. It is possible that Paul means to say that his true reason for imprisonment had become known to these officials and to *the public at large* (he actually says 'all the others'); but he may simply be referring to others concerned in his case.

17. The Greek does not make it quite clear what was happening. *Meaning to stir up fresh trouble for me as I lie in prison* could also be translated 'meaning to make use of my imprisonment to stir up fresh trouble'.

19. *Deliverance* is ambiguous, perhaps deliberately: either release from prison or final vindication at the Day of Christ Jesus. The whole phrase is a quotation of Job 13: 16 from the Greek Old Testament and, like many such, is used more for its familiar associations than for its precise significance. *The spirit of Jesus Christ* is a unique expression, and perhaps refers to the promise of Jesus that his disciples, when arrested and on trial, will not need to worry about their defence because the Holy Spirit will prompt their speech (Mark 13: 11).

21. At this point Paul's language becomes sketchy and broken as he holds two possibilities in mind. It is not easy to be sure of his meaning. *Life is Christ, and death gain* could be helped out by what he says later ('the gain of knowing Christ Jesus my Lord', 3: 8) and hence paraphrased thus: 'For me life means communion with Christ; death will mean more intimate communion with him.' This may indeed be in his mind, but it is difficult to see why such a piece of personal religion should appear in this particular context. It is perhaps better to interpret in this way: 'Life will mean letting *the greatness of Christ shine out clearly in my person*; death will do it even better.'

23. Paul's most vivid way of expressing his relation to Christ is to say, 'I have been crucified with Christ' (Gal. 2: 20). In this present letter, he longs 'to share his sufferings, in growing conformity with his death' (3: 10). But clearly he is now moving away from symbolic language, which expresses an inward denial of self, to a realistic imitation of Jesus. When he says he would *like to depart and be with Christ* he is thinking of a martyr's death like his, knowing full well that sharing his sufferings will bring 'the power of his resurrection' (3: 10). From these words it is scarcely possible to draw any more precise conclusions about the Christian's state between the time he dies and the final Day of Christ. ✶

UNITY AND OBEDIENCE

Only, let your conduct be worthy of the gospel of Christ, 27 so that whether I come and see you for myself or hear about you from a distance, I may know that you are standing firm, one in spirit, one in mind, contending as one man for the gospel faith, meeting your opponents 28 without so much as a tremor. This is a sure sign to them that their doom is sealed, but a sign of your salvation, and one afforded by God himself; for you have been granted 29

the privilege not only of believing in Christ but also of
30 suffering for him. You and I are engaged in the same
contest; you saw me in it once, and, as you hear, I am
in it still.

2 If then our common life in Christ yields anything to stir
the heart, any loving consolation, any sharing of the
2 Spirit, any warmth of affection or compassion, fill up my
cup of happiness by thinking and feeling alike, with the
same love for one another, the same turn of mind, and a
3 common care for unity. Rivalry and personal vanity
should have no place among you, but you should humbly
4 reckon others better than yourselves. You must look to
each other's interest and not merely to your own.

5   Let your bearing towards one another arise out of your
6 life in Christ Jesus. For the divine nature was his from the
first; yet he did not think to snatch at equality with God,
7 but made himself nothing, assuming the nature of a
8 slave. Bearing the human likeness, revealed in human
shape, he humbled himself, and in obedience accepted
9 even death—death on a cross. Therefore God raised him
to the heights and bestowed on him the name above all
10 names, that at the name of Jesus every knee should bow—
11 in heaven, on earth, and in the depths—and every
tongue confess, 'Jesus Christ is Lord', to the glory of God
the Father.

12   So you too, my friends, must be obedient, as always;
even more, now that I am away, than when I was with
you. You must work out your own salvation in fear and
13 trembling; for it is God who works in you, inspiring both
the will and the deed, for his own chosen purpose.

14   Do all you have to do without complaint or wrangling.

Show yourselves guileless and above reproach, faultless 15
children of God in a warped and crooked generation, in
which you shine like stars in a dark world and proffer the 16
word of life. Thus you will be my pride on the Day of
Christ, proof that I did not run my race in vain, or work
in vain. But if my life-blood is to crown that sacrifice 17
which is the offering up of your faith, I am glad of it, and
I share my gladness with you all. Rejoice, you no less 18
than I, and let us share our joy.

✻ This long section is a sustained appeal for unity and harmony in a church somewhat beset by rivalry and personal
vanity. There are several grounds of Paul's appeal to his
readers: their respect for the apostle, the impression they make
on the heathen, their gratitude for being Christians, and—
most important of all—the model provided by Christ (in
verses 5–11). This last passage raises the most difficult questions
in the letter, to many of which there are no certain answers.
Here are the main points.

(*a*) Verses 6–11, especially in Greek, have the arrangement
and style of poetry and can easily be printed in verse form. It
is generally agreed that *death on a cross* breaks the rhythm, and is
to be regarded as a comment on the preceding word. Other
comments may have been added to an original hymn, and
there are various ways of dividing it into two or three stanzas.
Here is one arrangement:

STANZA I
1. For the divine nature was his from the first;
2. Yet he did not think to snatch at equality with God,
3.   but made himself nothing,
4.   assuming the nature of a slave.
5. Bearing the human likeness,
6.   revealed in human shape,
7.   he humbled himself,

8.   and in obedience accepted even death
9.   —death on a cross.

STANZA 2

1.   Therefore God raised him to the heights
2.   and bestowed on him the name above all names,
3.   that at the name of Jesus
4.   every knee should bow—
5.   in heaven, on earth, and in the depths—
6.   and every tongue confess
7.   'Jesus Christ is Lord',
8.   to the glory of God the Father.

If the hymn was not first composed for this letter, then presumably its original setting was the Church's worship.

(*b*) The hymn contains some words not found elsewhere in the New Testament and ideas not characteristically Pauline e.g. the exaltation of Jesus is emphasized, not his resurrection; and he becomes Lord of the whole world, not only of the Church. Hence it is possible that Paul quoted or adapted an already existing hymn, or incorporated into his letter a hymn composed by one of his associates.

(*c*) It is difficult to know the exact meaning intended by some words in the hymn, especially in the earlier part, and the context must be allowed to decide. But this too is a matter of doubt. The general meaning of the whole hymn is sufficiently clear: it speaks of Christ's humiliation and exaltation. When, however, it is asked how particular phrases contribute to this theme, there is room for wide differences of opinion. There is no agreement among scholars about the sort of thinking that gave rise to this pattern of humiliation and exaltation, whether it was basically Jewish or Greek.

(*d*) Some see a Jewish background to the hymn because the humiliation section recalls the suffering Servant of the Lord in Isa. 52: 13 — 53: 12; and it is suggested that the early Church began to find a theological explanation of what Jesus did by supposing that he performed the task assigned by God

22

to his obedient Servant. There is obviously a general sympathy between stanza 1 (lines 3–8) and Isaiah's Servant; but they are not so closely related in detail (when compared in Greek) as to give convincing proof that the Servant was directly in mind when these lines were being composed. Moreover, it is still less convincing to suggest that stanza 2 came from this source, and stanza 1 (line 1) is not accounted for at all. Hence the total pattern of the hymn is not explained.

It is also suggested, by those who find the background of the hymn in Judaism, that its pattern derives from teaching about Adam. In 1 Cor. 15: 22 Paul says, 'As in Adam all men die, so in Christ all will be brought to life,' where 'Adam' stands for humanity subject to death, and 'Christ' for a new humanity offering the possibility of life. There is another fruitful comparison and contrast between Adam and Christ in Rom. 5: 12–19. Hence it is possible that Christ is portrayed in the hymn as the New Adam, who reversed the disobedience of the first Adam, *did not think to snatch at equality with God* (as Adam did when he listened to the tempting promise 'You will be like God', Gen. 3: 5 R.S.V.), and so was duly exalted to that lordship over the creation which the first Adam was intended to have, but forfeited. Again, it is true that such ideas are not alien to the general thought of the hymn, but it requires a rather specialized interpretation of key words if direct influence is to be proved.

Another suggestion opposes Christ not to Adam but to Satan. According to Jewish legend, in a book which may possibly come from the first century A.D., the devil refused to worship the image of God in newly created Adam. He defied God and said, 'If He be wroth with me, I will set my seat above the stars of heaven and will be like the highest.' Hence he and his angels were banished from heaven to earth (*Life of Adam and Eve* 12–15, a later embroidery of the ancient myth preserved in Isa. 14: 12–15). So, on this interpretation, the heavenly being, Christ, also leaves heaven for earth—but as a voluntary act and in obedience to God, not defiantly and unwillingly.

Such an explanation would occur only to someone acquainted with Jewish legend, and there is no reason to suppose that the Philippians were. Even if the hymn was composed in Jewish-Christian circles, Paul recites it for Gentile Christians. If the hymn had been written into 2 Thessalonians it would have been natural to contrast what is said of Christ with 'the man doomed to perdition' who 'rises in his pride against every god, so called, every object of men's worship, and even takes his seat in the temple of God claiming to be a god himself' (2 Thess. 2: 4). But such imagery is not attached to the Day of Christ in Philippians and scarcely suggests itself in the hymn.

(*e*) In seeking a Jewish background we have already looked at myths. Many scholars would agree that this is the right place to look, except that they turn to hellenistic myths rather than to Jewish. (The word 'hellenistic' is used of the life and culture of Greek-speaking lands from the time of Alexander the Great onwards—he died in 323 B.C.—when Greek influence gripped Egypt and the Near East, and conversely Egyptian and Oriental ideas were interfused with Greek thinking.) On this view, the hymn draws upon a widely diffused myth (possibly originating in the religion of Persia) of a Divine Redeemer who descends from heaven to earth and the underworld, discloses himself to those who are to be redeemed, and then triumphantly ascends. In one form the myth speaks of a Heavenly Man who existed with God from the very first but fell a prey to opposing forces and descended to this lower world. Though rescued by God and restored to his earlier condition, he left behind in this lower world a portion of his being. From this remnant of the Heavenly Man human beings are descended, and so in part are aliens in this lower world. They belong in essence to the heavenly world, and therefore must be rescued by the descent of the Heavenly Man-Redeemer and re-ascend with him.

Such a myth, of course, does not pretend to describe observable events; it is a symbolic method of describing man's

relation to this life and the reality that lies beyond. Some of this kind best fits the pattern of the hymn and woul well within the experience of the Philippians; but it is o to two serious objections. The myth of the descending l deemer is a good deal plainer in scholars' reconstructions o from documents written later than the New Testament tha it is in any writing of Paul's time or earlier; and the hymn not in any obvious way concerned with the redemption o humanity but with the honour to be given to Christ Jesus.

(*f*) This last observation perhaps suggests how the hymn ought to be understood as part of Paul's letter to the Philippians. It is intended to set out not a doctrine of redemption or even a doctrine of incarnation but the sort of honour that is due to Christ. It is the same kind of hymn as those that are sung in the Revelation of John: 'Thou art worthy, O Lord our God, to receive glory and honour and power, because thou didst create all things; by thy will they were created, and have their being!'...'Worthy is the Lamb, the Lamb that was slain, to receive all power and wealth, wisdom and might, honour and glory and praise!' (Rev. 4: 11; 5: 12). In Philippians, however, the honour is not given to the creator or to the sacrificial Lamb but to the one who was made Lord of all the powers *in heaven, on earth, and in the depths* after he had first submitted himself to them. The hymn follows a very ancient tradition for acclaiming Near Eastern kings—first addressing them as divine persons, then praising their graciousness in visiting their people and acting for their benefit, and finally describing the universal praise that is their due. This acclamation pattern derives from ancient mythology, but the myth that underlies it is not necessarily active in the mind of anyone using it in worship. In itself it provides the proper style for ascribing honour, and there is no more to it than that. But when we observe the kind of honour that is ascribed to Jesus Christ, sooner or later we are compelled to ask questions about the relation of Christ to God and to mankind, and so worship leads to theology. Teaching about the Suffering Servant, the

Last Adam and even the fall of Satan may then suggest ways of examining these questions; but in Paul's day the process had only begun. The hymn to Christ does not directly answer the theological questions of a later time when a fully developed doctrine of Christ had been established, though it is part of the evidence on which such a doctrine relies.

27–30. This appeal uses imagery drawn from the city state (*let your conduct* appears in R.V. margin as 'behave as citizens', though that over-presses the Greek), from the soldier's life (*standing firm*), and from the athletic contests which played an important part in Greek life and religion (*contending, contest*). Hence the religious word *salvation* suits this language if it is understood as 'victory'. If the Philippian Christians resist all attacks, it will be an indication to their opponents that the non-Christians cannot win.

2: 1–4. This is a fine rhetorical passage in which the chief words could have more than one interpretation. It is a many-sided appeal for unity based on the Philippians' experience of living in a Christian community. The closing sentence could equally well mean 'You must consider each other's qualities and not merely your own'. The word *humbly*, which is echoed at verse 8 by 'he humbled himself', introduces a very important Christian moral attitude, though it is open to exploitation and self-deception if it is thought of merely as self-depreciation. In Greek life the word translated *humbly* meant the subservient attitude of a lower-class person; in Christianity, by reflection on the work of Christ, it was used to mean the lowly service done by a noble person.

2: 5. This verse is somewhat abbreviated in the Greek: literally it is 'Have that bearing towards one another which also is in Christ Jesus'. If *in Christ Jesus* is given its normal meaning (namely, belonging to Christ's people), the N.E.B. translation results; otherwise, the N.E.B. footnote completes the second half of the sentence with 'which was also found in Christ Jesus'.

2: 6–8   THE HYMN TO CHRIST: STANZA I

2: 6. *The divine nature was his from the first* is far superior to the conventional translation 'being originally in the form of God'. The Greek word *morphe*, in philosophical writing, meant the form that corresponds to the underlying reality; but in a hymn like this, it has the same general meaning as *nature*. It conveys a strong impression of Christ's intimate relation to God, without giving it precise or formal definition. Some scholars have suggested that *morphe* is equivalent to *eikon*, meaning image, so that Christ is not said to possess the divine *nature* but to be 'in the image of God' like Adam. This answers the question why, if he already possessed the divine nature, he could *think to snatch at equality with God*; but no-one has suggested why *morphe* should have been used if *eikon* was intended.

He did not think to snatch at equality with God is the most perplexing phrase in the hymn, and is the chief source of the contrast with Adam and with Satan already mentioned. Is *equality with God* a higher dignity than *the divine nature*? Since Christ renounced it at this stage, was he rewarded with it for his obedience? Or does *equality with God* suggest an exercise of the divine powers which was possible for him (since he possessed *the divine nature*), but which he renounced until he had earned it by his obedience? Most probably it suggests nothing of the sort: *equality with God* and *the divine nature* are equivalent phrases (as is very natural in such a hymn—compare the repetitions in lines 3 and 4, 5 and 6 of this stanza). They are not intended to raise or answer this kind of theological question. The real difficulty lies in the Greek word *harpagmos* which means a prize to be seized or to be held tight, or even a piece of good fortune. If it means 'a prize to be seized', then the N.E.B. translation follows; and it is necessary to add 'for his own benefit' to make sense of it. If it has one of the other meanings, then the translation of the N.E.B. footnote is possible: 'yet he did not prize his equality with God', i.e.

he did not hold it tight but renounced it for the benefit of others.

2: 7–9. It is generally supposed that *made himself nothing* (line 3) refers to the Incarnation, i.e. to Jesus' appearance on earth as a helpless child, who became a man with many of the normal human limitations, lived in obedience to God, and was crucified. Those who press the parallel with the Servant of the Lord in Isaiah translate instead 'he poured himself out' ('he poured out his soul to death', Isa. 53: 12, though the Greek Old Testament has quite different wording from Paul's), and make the statement refer to Christ's death. The more general language of the N.E.B. is preferable, but the whole description of these verses is probably not intended to be a summary of the impression made by Jesus in the gospel narratives, but a forceful evocation of his position as *slave* in contrast with his position as *Lord*. All the phrases for his slavery, humiliation and obedience mean that he willingly accepted the human condition of powerlessness and mortality (compare 'the shackles of mortality' in Rom. 8: 21), whereas the rest of us are unwilling victims.

2: 9–11   THE HYMN TO CHRIST: STANZA 2

2: 9–11. The triumphant conclusion of the acclamation (lines 4 to 8 of this stanza) is modelled on God's promise in Isa. 45: 23, 25: 'To me every knee shall bow, every tongue shall swear...In the Lord all the offspring of Israel shall triumph and glory' (R.S.V.). The same passage is quoted in Rom. 14: 11 with the same difference from the Hebrew and the Greek Old Testament (*confess* or 'acknowledge' substituted for 'swear'); but here *in heaven, on earth, and in the depths* is inserted (line 5). This may be merely a symbol for the universality of the honour that is offered to Christ, but more probably is intended to suggest the unseen powers that influence human life, against which humanity often seems helpless. Jesus Christ, who is acknowledged as Lord over these powers, knows what it is to be subject to them. The words *Jesus Christ is Lord* (line 7) were the earliest and simplest confession of faith when people became Christian, and it is possible that the hymn was first used at baptism. In any case, it shows any Christian how great and universal is the Lord whom he honours when he makes his personal confession of faith. *At the name of Jesus* (line 3) does not mean that everyone should bow the knee when the actual name Jesus is mentioned, however appropriate that may be. It means that to Jesus is offered the honour that is proper only to God, because Jesus bears *the name above all names* (line 2), i.e. the name of God himself. To call God by a particular name would be to reduce him to something less than God. He cannot be named or classified. (Jews always avoided pronouncing the sacred name, even when it appeared as YHWH in scripture.) But in Jesus Christ there is someone who can be precisely named, through whom God can be genuinely known and worshipped. It is significant that this final stanza of the hymn lays all the stress, not on the heroic quality of Jesus, but on God's activity in exalting and acknowledging him.

2: 12–13. An appeal for continued obedience is coupled with an instruction to be independent. The Philippians *must be obedient* to the pattern of Christian life disclosed in the humility and exaltation of Christ; but the church itself *must work out* its own version of that pattern to a finally satisfying conclusion. (In this letter, the word *salvation* is a comprehensive word for the satisfactory conclusion of God's intentions for his people.) At the same time, they are to have a lively sense that they are free to act in this way only because God is at work in them. *Fear and trembling* is a phrase from Jewish piety, as in Ps. 2: 11: 'Serve the Lord with fear, and rejoice with trembling'; it indicates reverence and devotion.

2: 15. *A warped and crooked generation* is a quotation from the farewell song of Moses (Deut. 32: 5), where it is a rebuke to the Israelites; but Paul seems to be remembering the words rather than the original occasion. Instead of telling the

Philippians that they *shine like stars* he could be urging them to shine out like stars in a dark world, or indeed like stars in the sky. (The Greek simply has *kosmos* which usually means 'world', but can mean 'sky'—the N.E.B. footnote quaintly suggests 'firmament'.) Paul's intention is sufficiently clear, though there is a further ambiguity in the final words of the sentence. *The word of life* could obviously mean the life-giving word, that is, the Christian gospel; so that Christians are proffering the gospel to the world, or (with another possible translation of the verb) are themselves holding fast to it. But *word of life* could also be understood in the sense it would have in Johannine writings (compare I John I: I 'our theme is the word of life' with John I: I–5 where there are the same themes of word, life, light and darkness); and N.E.B. footnote suggests 'as the very principle of its life' instead of *and proffer the word of life*. But such a thought is scarcely in Paul's mind at this point: he is offering encouragement, not propounding theological truths in a nutshell.

2: 17. Paul now relinquishes the athletic metaphor ('run my race' in verse 16—it will be used again at 3: 12–14) and substitutes ritual language without making it quite plain what he means (nor does the N.E.B. translation). Literally, he says 'But even if I am poured out as a libation at the sacrifice and priestly ministry of your faith'. He compares his possible execution to a libation (which was a drink-offering poured on the ground in honour of the god) accompanying another sacrificial action. Either Paul himself is offering the Philippians' faith to God, or the Philippians are making the offering, perhaps their devotion and support for the apostle. He uses similar imprecise imagery in Rom. 15: 16: 'My priestly service is the preaching of the gospel of God, and it falls to me to offer the Gentiles to him as an acceptable sacrifice.' What matters to Paul is the general impression, not the details of sacrificial worship, in which he shows little interest. ✳

FUTURE PLANS

I hope (under the Lord Jesus) to send Timothy to you 19
soon; it will cheer me to hear news of you. There is no 20
one else here who sees things as I do, and takes a genuine
interest in your concerns; they are all bent on their own 21
ends, not on the cause of Christ Jesus. But Timothy's 22
record is known to you: you know that he has been at my
side in the service of the Gospel like a son working under
his father. Timothy, then, I hope to send as soon as ever I 23
can see how things are going with me; and I am confident, 24
under the Lord, that I shall myself be coming before long.

I feel also I must send our brother Epaphroditus, my 25
fellow-worker and comrade, whom you commissioned
to minister to my needs. He has been missing all of you 26
sadly, and has been distressed that you heard he was ill.
(He was indeed dangerously ill, but God was merciful to 27
him, and merciful no less to me, to spare me sorrow upon
sorrow.) For this reason I am all the more eager to send 28
him, to give you the happiness of seeing him again, and
to relieve my sorrow. Welcome him then in the fellow- 29
ship of the Lord with whole-hearted delight. You should
honour men like him; in Christ's cause he came near to 30
death, risking his life to render me the service you could
not give.

✻ Epaphroditus, who is otherwise unknown, had been entrusted by the Philippian Church with their gift for Paul. To
carry out his responsibility he had risked his life and become
dangerously ill. Whether this happened on his way to Paul or
after his arrival, we do not know. He was, however, upset
that news of his illness should have gone to Philippi, and so
Paul sends him back as bearer of this letter.

31

As soon as Paul knows how his own affair is turning out, he intends to send Timothy to visit the Church and report back. Timothy is obviously Paul's most trusted helper and the only one he can rely on. He accompanied Paul on the journey to Europe recorded in Acts 16 and the following chapters, and helped to found the church at Philippi. He is named as the joint author with Paul of 1 Thessalonians, 2 Thessalonians, 2 Corinthians, Colossians, Philemon, and Philippians; and is mentioned in 1 Corinthians and Romans. Two Pastoral Letters are addressed to him. It is not surprising that Paul says *There is no one else here who sees things as I do* or (as it could be translated) 'There is no one else here like him'. It has already been suggested (on page 17) that the comment in verse 21 springs from Paul's feeling that other leaders are now taking it for granted that he can no longer exercise effective control of the Christian mission. ✳

LOSS AND GAIN

3 And now, friends, farewell; I wish you joy in the Lord.
   To repeat what I have written to you before is no
2 trouble to me, and it is a safeguard for you. Beware of those dogs and their malpractices. Beware of those who insist on mutilation—'circumcision' I will not call it;
3 we are the circumcised, we whose worship is spiritual, whose pride is in Christ Jesus, and who put no confidence
4 in anything external. Not that I am without grounds myself even for confidence of that kind. If anyone thinks to base his claims on externals, I could make a stronger case
5 for myself: circumcised on my eighth day, Israelite by race, of the tribe of Benjamin, a Hebrew born and bred;
6 in my attitude to the law, a Pharisee; in pious zeal, a
7 persecutor of the church; in legal rectitude, faultless. But
8 all such assets I have written off because of Christ. I

would say more: I count everything sheer loss, because all is far outweighed by the gain of knowing Christ Jesus my Lord, for whose sake I did in fact lose everything. I count it so much garbage, for the sake of gaining Christ and finding myself incorporate in him, with no righteous- 9 ness of my own, no legal rectitude, but the righteousness which comes from faith in Christ, given by God in re- sponse to faith. All I care for is to know Christ, to ex- 10 perience the power of his resurrection, and to share his sufferings, in growing conformity with his death, if only 11 I may finally arrive at the resurrection from the dead.

It is not to be thought that I have already achieved all 12 this. I have not yet reached perfection, but I press on, hoping to take hold of that for which Christ once took hold of me. My friends, I do not reckon myself to have 13 got hold of it yet. All I can say is this: forgetting what is behind me, and reaching out for that which lies ahead, I 14 press towards the goal to win the prize which is God's call to the life above, in Christ Jesus.

Let us then keep to this way of thinking, those of us 15 who are mature. If there is any point on which you think differently, this also God will make plain to you. Only 16 let our conduct be consistent with the level we have already reached.

Agree together, my friends, to follow my example. 17 You have us for a model; watch those whose way of life conforms to it. For, as I have often told you, and now tell 18 you with tears in my eyes, there are many whose way of life makes them enemies of the cross of Christ. They are 19 heading for destruction, appetite is their god, and they glory in their shame. Their minds are set on earthly

20 things. We, by contrast, are citizens of heaven, and from heaven we expect our deliverer to come, the Lord Jesus
21 Christ. He will transfigure the body belonging to our humble state, and give it a form like that of his own resplendent body, by the very power which enables him
4 to make all things subject to himself. Therefore, my friends, beloved friends whom I long for, my joy, my crown, stand thus firm in the Lord, my beloved!

* At this point in the letter a very noticeable change takes place. It looks as if Paul is about to finish with suitable fare-well messages—the sort of thing he in fact says at 4: 4–9—but instead, he launches into sharply worded warnings and a highly personal statement of his own religious journey. He denounces opponents who cannot be identified from what has gone before, and the situation about which he speaks is different from that presupposed earlier in the letter. In talking about *the righteousness which comes from faith in Christ* as well as about sharing his death and resurrection, he is echoing main themes of Galatians and Romans and his recital of Jewish privileges has a further parallel in 2 Cor. 11: 21–2.

For such reasons, many scholars are persuaded that 3: 2 — 4: 1 does not belong to the present letter, but is part of Paul's correspondence with the church on another occasion (see pages 3–4). Against this view it can be argued that abrupt changes of mood are found in other Pauline letters, that opponents are already in mind as early as 1: 28, and that the argument from Paul's personal experience fits the general approach of this letter particularly well. If 3: 1 — 4: 1 is regarded as really belonging to the present letter, it must be supposed that Paul, having spoken to the church about its inner tensions, now turns to the last things he wants to say to them about pressures from outside. In so doing, he uses arguments from stock—though with fresh urgency and feeling.

It is difficult to discover who the opponents were, and

34

whether those called *dogs* in 3: 2 are the same as the *enemies of the cross of Christ* in 3: 18–19. Some scholars think that two groups of people are attacked, since they are accused of such opposite faults in the two places. But there is no other indication to suggest that Paul has abandoned one set of opponents for another, and the most natural reading of the whole passage suggests that he is emotionally involved with the same problem throughout. Hence it is important to notice that he is not calmly listing the dangerous errors of these opponents but abusing them. His language tells us what he feels about them, and is not direct evidence of their thought and practices.

At the beginning of the passage, the vigorous remarks about circumcision make it clear that the opponents advocate Jewish ritual practices. Paul's insistence that he was *in legal rectitude, faultless* suggests that they set great store by the Mosaic law; and his emphatic claim to be Jewish by birth suggests that they were not. When, in verse 12, he admits that he has *not yet reached perfection*, it is likely that the opponents either claimed that they had or that, in Jewish law and ritual, they had a means for reaching it. Since Paul puts considerable stress on *knowing Christ Jesus my Lord* (in verses 8 and 10), it is possible that the opponents shared some features of a varied and widespread religious movement that regarded 'knowledge' (Greek *gnosis* or techniques of religious insight) as the certain way of reaching perfection. They may have been Jews who had adapted their religion to Greek patterns, but such opponents would scarcely have been a serious attraction to Christians. It is more likely that their religion included Christian features, and it is possible that they were Jewish-Christian propagandists, intent on making members of a Gentile church into complete Christians by circumcision and obedience to the law. Such propaganda is familiar from Galatians. But the tone of Paul's remarks in this letter suggests that he is fighting neither against his own people nor against fellow-Christians, but against a persuasive religious group who had made a 'way of perfection' out of Greek, Jewish, and Christian elements. Such a group might well be regarded by Paul as *enemies of the cross of Christ*, calling out his strongest invective.

1. Most translations simply give 'rejoice in the Lord', but the Greek word *chairete* (rejoice) is a common way of saying *farewell*. Paul uses the word again at 4: 4 and there, in accordance with the mood of this letter, stresses the literal meaning. Hence the N.E.B. expresses both rejoicing and farewell.

The second half of the verse might conceivably refer to the repeated rejoicing of this letter, but Paul would scarcely justify the repetition as a safeguard. If 3: 2 — 4: 1 were detached as part of another letter, then 3: 1 would join up with 4: 2, and Paul would be repeating his appeal for unity by directly addressing two women who had quarrelled. According to the N.E.B. translation, however, the section 3: 2 — 4: 1 contains a repeated statement of warnings given in previous letters. This may be supported by 'as I have often told you' at 3: 18, and suggests that part of Paul's correspondence with Philippi has not been preserved.

2. Every people has its conventions about using animal names as insults. *Dogs* are always mentioned with contempt in the Old Testament as unclean animals (presumably because they were scavengers and savage), and so provided the Jews with an insulting name for Gentiles. Paul uses it of people who subvert the faith, and adds that they are 'malicious workers'—which may be a reference to *their malpractices*; but may mean that they are propagandists, since 'worker' became a standard term for a missionary.

3. To the Jew, circumcision was the distinctive external sign of belonging to the People of God. Paul believes that 'circumcision has value, provided you keep the law; but if you break the law, then your circumcision is as if it had never been. Equally, if an uncircumcised man keeps the precepts of the law, will he not count as circumcised?...The true Jew is not he who is such in externals, neither is the true circumcision the external mark in the flesh. The true Jew is he who

is such inwardly, and the true circumcision is of the heart, directed not by written precepts but by the Spirit' (Rom. 2: 25–29). This develops Old Testament teaching found in Deuteronomy and Jeremiah in the light of Paul's belief that the Holy Spirit was a guarantee of God's choice of a new people in Christ, just as circumcision was the guarantee of the choice of his original people in Abraham. Hence the contrast between the *external* (which gives the proper meaning in this place of Paul's highly individual use of the word 'flesh') and the *spiritual*—though in fact all manuscripts except one have either 'who worship God in the spirit' or 'who worship by the Spirit of God'. Neither in this context nor elsewhere does Paul speak with contempt of circumcision, even though in Gal. 5: 6 he says that 'if we are in union with Christ Jesus circumcision makes no difference at all'. When, therefore, he says that the opponents 'insist on mutilation' and refuses to call it circumcision, it sounds as if he is not talking about genuine Jewish convictions at all, but about a heathen amalgam of rites and ideas.

5–6. *Circumcised on my eighth day*, according to the rule in Lev. 12: 3; *Israelite by race*, not a convert; *of the tribe of Benjamin* which produced Saul, the first Israelite King (Paul's Jewish name was Saul); *a Hebrew born and bred* or possibly 'a Hebrew-speaking Jew of a Hebrew-speaking family'. As a *Pharisee*, he belonged to a powerful religious movement which existed to serve God by strict practice of the law (not only the written commands but also the body of traditional interpretations) in every department of life. Pharisees formed themselves into small groups for study and devotion, pledged themselves to special rules of purification and tithing, and were active in spreading their piety by teaching and example. In Gal. 1: 14 Paul says that he outstripped many of his Jewish contemporaries in his boundless devotion to the traditions of his ancestors. It is not surprising that a man of such *pious zeal* should have persecuted the breakaway Christian movement; and it is entirely in agreement with Pharisaic

convictions that he should have thought himself *in legal recti-*
tude, faultless, i.e. he practised the strict Pharisaic code
exactly and without fault.

7–9. These verses describe the revolution when the Pharisee
became a Christian. He is still urgently concerned with dis-
covering how anyone can stand in right relationship to God.
(This is the meaning of the Greek word translated both by
'rectitude' and by *righteousness*; it is exceedingly difficult to
suggest an English equivalent, and these are more misleading
than helpful.) As a Pharisee, he believed that God had disclosed his will in the law, and had given men the ability to
interpret it and the power to do it. Therefore anyone who
completely obeyed the law must be in right relationship to
God. But this train of reasoning made him a 'persecutor of
the church' which he now believes to be the body in which
God's will is truly performed. Therefore his Jewish grounding
and his Pharisaic piety are not a guarantee of right relation to
God but the great barrier to it. It is therefore renounced and
replaced by *knowing Christ Jesus my Lord.*

This change in Paul's understanding of 'righteousness' is
the main subject of Rom. 1–8 and a large part of Galatians.
There too, the word *faith* is of central importance, especially
in the conviction that a man is justified (or put in right relation with God) by faith, quite apart from success in keeping
the law (Rom. 3: 28). At the centre of Pharisaic piety there
stood faithfulness to the law—this was the way to communion
with God; indeed keeping the law was itself communion
with him. At the centre of Paul's Christian piety stood *faith,*
that is, acceptance of communion with God, which God
freely offers in Christ even to an enemy of the truth like Paul
the Pharisee. Therefore religious zeal and strict obedience
cannot confer a right to this communion, and so they are
dismissed.

10–11. *To know Christ* has some precedent in common
Hebrew usage, where the verb 'to know' can mean 'to have
close personal knowledge of'. It is also related to Old Testa-

ment language about knowledge of God, which means not only knowledge of his existence and nature, but much more of his will. Thus in Jer. 31: 33–4, the promise that 'I will put my law within them, and I will write it upon their hearts; and I will be their God, and they shall be my people' is at once explained by 'no longer shall each man teach his neighbour and each his brother, saying "know the Lord", for they shall all know me'. But Paul's knowledge of Christ goes beyond all this to sharing in Christ's sufferings and experiencing his resurrection. The believer is identified with Christ. This kind of knowledge is akin to, though not the same as, the *gnosis* that was offered in some Greek religions of salvation. To express the new religious experience which came to him in Christ, Paul extended traditional Jewish language by ideas from Greek religion.

No doubt he is thinking partly of mystical experience, perhaps such as he had at his conversion and certainly later. In Rom. 6: 3–4 he explained entry into the church by baptism as participation in Christ's death and being set on the new path of life. Therefore this is the condition of any Christian, whether he has mystical experiences or not; and it is worked out in the decisions that Christians must constantly make. If Paul is indeed facing the possibility of execution, the words have sharp point—though everything he suffered brought him into *growing conformity* with Christ's death. *The resurrection from the dead* is the final goal, put in traditional words, of those who are already identified with Christ.

12–14. Certain Greek religions promised *perfection* to the initiates; that is, by rituals and secret knowledge they could be transformed into a condition of complete religious attainment (whatever that meant). Paul perhaps takes the word from the propaganda of the opponents, in order to deny that Christianity is nothing more than another technique for achieving such results. In his view, the Christian life is a progressive discovery of what it means to have been grasped by Christ. Its *goal* is therefore nothing else than Christ himself.

15. *Mature* could also be translated 'perfect'. Paul either deliberately plays on the two possibilities, or he means 'those of us who are attracted by the perfection propaganda'.

18–19. Those who think that these *enemies* are different from the 'dogs' of verse 2 usually regard them as Christians who have broken out into rather shocking behaviour. The description of their faults is disappointingly vague. *Appetite is their god* may mean that they are excessively greedy for food (the common translation is 'their god is the belly'), but it is ludicrous to imagine Paul shedding tears about that. It is better to suppose that he is showing his disgust for propaganda, partly Jewish and partly gnostic, that degrades the Christian religion when it tries to absorb it.

20. Paul uses the commonplace contrast of earthly and heavenly, freshened up by a piece of political imagery, to say that the religion of the opponents is a purely human creation, whereas Christianity arises from the activity and intervention of God. (Jewish writers constantly used 'heaven' as a way of talking about God.) The divine intervention is described in language taken from the Day of Christ, though the unusual word *deliverer* is used. There is something very similar in 1 Thess. 1: 10 where Christians 'wait expectantly for the appearance from heaven of his Son Jesus...our deliverer from the terrors of judgement to come'; but different Greek words are translated *deliverer* in the two passages. There it is *ruomenos* (see page 65); here it is *soter*, commonly translated 'saviour'. Although Paul talks of 'salvation' as the final condition of Christians and uses the verb 'to save' quite freely, and although 'Saviour' was used of God in the Old Testament, Paul does not elsewhere apply this title to Jesus (except that it is found in Ephesians and the Pastoral Letters which are possibly not from Paul's hand). In the Greek world it was a common name for the god of a cult, and Roman emperors were addressed by this title. It is possible that Paul deliberately chose it here to counter the claims of the rival propaganda.

21. What will happen to Christians at the Day of Christ is

described in language more symbolic than literal, and taken from the extended treatment in the Corinthian letters. It is presumed that the risen Christ exists in *his own resplendent body* (literally, 'the body suited to his glory'). At the arrival of the deliverer, our bodies *belonging to our humble state* will be changed to match his. Similarly in 1 Cor. 15: 43, when speaking of the resurrection of the dead, Paul says, 'Sown in humiliation, it is raised in glory.' Such language is symbolic because it is not intended to give information about the future disposal of human bone and muscle, but to indicate a trans-formation of human existence. Paul often uses the word *body*, in his own special sense, to mean a man's whole self, neither ignoring nor over-emphasizing his physical nature, and some-times stressing his corporate existence. Here he means that ordinary human existence (which is *humble* because imperfect, impermanent, and subject to suffering) will be brought into line with Christ's existence. 'As we have worn the likeness of the man made of dust, so we shall wear the likeness of the heavenly man' (1 Cor. 15: 49). The present verse has close parallels, in the Greek words and in the thought, with 2: 7-11; this may be deliberate. At the Day of Christ it will be possible to say of Christians what there was said of Christ himself. *

FINAL APPEALS

I beg Euodia, and I beg Syntyche, to agree together in the 2
Lord's fellowship. Yes, and you too, my loyal comrade, 3
I ask you to help these women, who shared my struggles
in the cause of the Gospel, with Clement and my other
fellow-workers, whose names are in the book of life.

Farewell; I wish you all joy in the Lord. I will say it 4
again: all joy be yours.

Let your magnanimity be manifest to all. 5

The Lord is near; have no anxiety, but in everything 6

make your requests known to God in prayer and petition
7 with thanksgiving. Then the peace of God, which is
beyond our utmost understanding, will keep guard over
your hearts and your thoughts, in Christ Jesus.

8   And now, my friends, all that is true, all that is noble,
all that is just and pure, all that is lovable and gracious,
whatever is excellent and admirable—fill all your thoughts
with these things.

9   The lessons I taught you, the tradition I have passed on,
all that you heard me say or saw me do, put into practice;
and the God of peace will be with you.

* 2–3. The disagreement between the two women helps to
ruin *the Lord's fellowship*, and gives added force to the appeal
for a common mind in 1: 27 — 2: 18. Nothing more is
known about the people mentioned. *The book of life* is a
common Old Testament symbol for God's recognition of
those who belong to him, and appears in several passages of
Revelation (3: 5; 13: 8; 20: 15).

6. *The Lord is near* could be another example of the link
between prayer and the expectation of Christ's early return;
but it could also be an echo of Ps. 145: 18 R.S.V.: 'The Lord
is near to all who call upon him.'

7. When Paul speaks of 'the God of peace' (as in verse 9), it
is usually because the unity and harmony of the church are
threatened (as at 2 Thess. 3: 16). *The peace of God* is the
peace he brings to such a situation. It is said to be *beyond our
utmost understanding* (or possibly of far more worth than
human reasoning) because Paul also has in mind the final
reconciliation of all enmities and contradictions at the Day of
Christ.

8. Consequently it is possible to anticipate the final *peace of
God* by filling *all your thoughts* with the things that promote
harmony and unity. All the qualities mentioned, and indeed

the teaching device of reciting such lists of good qualities, are taken from popular moral teaching of Paul's day (particularly that of the Stoic philosophers who, in Paul's day, were well represented by the famous writer and politician, Seneca). It has been suggested that Paul was urging his readers to recognize what was good in the morals of pagan society; but it is more likely that he expects them to discover these qualities in their own Christian 'tradition'. ✳

GRATITUDE FOR A GIFT

It is a great joy to me, in the Lord, that after so long your 10 care for me has now blossomed afresh. You did care about me before for that matter; it was opportunity that you lacked. Not that I am alluding to want, for I have learned 11 to find resources in myself whatever my circumstances. I 12 know what it is to be brought low, and I know what it is to have plenty. I have been very thoroughly initiated into the human lot with all its ups and downs—fullness and hunger, plenty and want. I have strength for anything 13 through him who gives me power. But it was kind of you 14 to share the burden of my troubles.

As you know yourselves, Philippians, in the early days 15 of my mission, when I set out from Macedonia, you were the only congregation that were my partners in payments and receipts; for even at Thessalonica you contributed to 16 my needs, not once but twice over. Do not think I set my 17 heart upon the gift; all I care for is the profit accruing to you. However, here I give you my receipt for everything 18 —for more than everything; I am paid in full, now that I have received from Epaphroditus what you sent. It is a fragrant offering, an acceptable sacrifice, pleasing to God.

19 And my God will supply all your wants out of the
20 magnificence of his riches in Christ Jesus. To our God and
Father be glory for endless ages! Amen.

* It is surprising to find such an elaborate, carefully worded
expression of thanks coming not only at the end of the letter,
but also after the miscellaneous section 4: 2–9. Some have
supposed that it is really a separate letter of thanks sent earlier
when the gift was received; or it may have been a special
acknowledgement sent to the 'bishops and deacons' (1: 1) if
they had a special responsibility for church finance. But
there may have been good reasons why Paul felt it necessary
to deal first with internal dissensions and a rival religion before
combining defensiveness and warm appreciation in his *receipt
for everything*. If the church was not unanimous in approving
the gift, because some thought that Paul was like the propagandists who made money out of religion, it might meet
the case; but this is no more than a guess.

10–14. Paul expresses his gratitude while insisting that he
does not solicit gifts and can do without them (an awkward
thing to say in a letter of thanks!). Perhaps deliberately, he
adopts two pieces of jargon. Like the Stoic philosopher he had
achieved independence of others (*resources in myself*), and like
the exponent of a religious cult he had been *initiated*—though
not into religious mysteries, but *into the human lot with all its
ups and downs*, i.e. he is not escaping from life into religion or
philosophy. He christianizes this borrowed language by
attributing his strength to *him who gives me power*.

15–19. He next recalls their help in the early days of his
European mission (as if to say that their present support is not
a new departure) and employs a number of commercial
terms (*payments and receipts, the profit accruing, my receipt, paid
in full*). This is something more than a natural way of saying
that they owe a great deal to him, and that the gift is much to
their credit. He seems to be insisting that what they have given
him is in payment for what he has given them. He is not

making money out of them, but they are *partners* in the Christian enterprise. Having made the point, he reverts to religious language—their gift is really an offering to God. ✳

CLOSE

Give my greetings, in the fellowship of Christ, to each 21 one of God's people. The brothers who are now with me send their greetings to you, and so do all God's people here, 22 particularly those who belong to the imperial establishment.

The grace of our Lord Jesus Christ be with your spirit. 23

✳ *The imperial establishment* is literally 'Caesar's household'. In Rome this would refer to members of the emperor's domestic and administrative staff; in the provinces it would mean officials managing the imperial property. Neither this reference, nor the *praetorium* in 1: 13, settles the place of Paul's imprisonment; but both show the spreading influence of the Christian faith. ✳

✳   ✳   ✳   ✳   ✳   ✳   ✳   ✳   ✳   ✳   ✳   ✳   ✳

THE SIGNIFICANCE OF THE LETTER

This highly personal document throws light on the most formidable of the early Christian leaders, especially if it was his last public letter. The many-sided character of Paul discloses new depths; and it is chiefly in its personal understanding of the Christian faith that the significance of this letter is to be found. It contains no new theological teaching, no fresh instruction in morals; but its exploration of the encounter between Christ, the Christian, and the world of human experience constitutes its claim on the modern reader.

In some of the other letters, and notably in the Thessalonian correspondence, Paul makes full use of language about the return of Christ, the final judgement, the resurrection of the dead, and so on. It has already been pointed out in the commentary that this language is still retained in Philippians; but it is now balanced at every point by equally impressive statements about the present condition of Christians and about life in the Church before the Day of Christ.

The Two Sides of Christian Life

Paul regards the Day of Christ as the guaranteed completion of the work that has now been begun by God in the Church and by the Church. But this conviction releases him for the work that must now be done. Even if Christians are taught to look somewhat into the distance for the completion of their aims, there is already a kind of fulfilment for them as they 'shine like stars in a dark world' (2: 15).

At the Day of Christ they will reap the reward of their obedience; but this does not devalue human existence at the present time. When Paul appeals to them by the enheartening qualities of their common life in Christ (2: 1), and when he tells them to fill all their thoughts with the noble virtues of human society (4: 8), he is balancing the present experience and the final fulfilment.

At the Day of Christ he expects proof that he has not lived and worked in vain. He runs his race with a lively sense of the prize to be won (and this is the kind of race in which all competitors can win—indeed, the more winners, the greater the prize). But it is clear that the actual running of the race is as enthralling as the winning of it. He hopes 'to take hold of that for which Christ once took hold of' him (3: 12)—which is something of a paradox. He means that he already has the experience of being held by Christ, and will finally complete it by grasping him himself.

He also expresses his hope by saying that he expects to arrive finally at the resurrection from the dead; but already he knows the power of Christ's resurrection (3: 10, 11). This means that, to serve Christ and to look after the churches, he encounters danger, undergoes suffering, sees his plans upset and his work frustrated, is misrepresented and abused—yet he emerges from all his trials with undiminished conviction and a new quality of joy.

At the end, the deliverer will come to transform 'the body belonging to our humble state, and give it a form like that of his own resplendent body' (3: 21). But plainly, the transformation is already taking place—in Paul's willing acceptance of humility. His imprisonment is a means of advancing the gospel, the jealousy of his rivals causes Christ to be proclaimed. His own death may honour Christ as much as—even more than—his strenuous missionary work. He has learnt to find resources in himself whatever his circumstances (4: 11). Already he is incorporate in Christ.

The Meaning of Christ

This balance between the present humble condition and the final triumph reflects, in Paul's life, what is said of Christ in the famous hymn of 2: 6–11. The commentary has already suggested that the hymn should be regarded as a way of expressing the honour that is due to Christ; but theologians have usually tried to go further and discover in it information about the 'nature' of Christ. The simplest and safest answer to their enquiry is to say that it was the nature of Christ to display this humiliation and exaltation, and to ground both in the being of God himself.

From that point onwards further theological questions can be raised; but it is unlikely that they will get a satisfactory answer if the questioners understand the language of the hymn in too literal a fashion. It has been suggested that the pattern of the hymn derives from a Near Eastern myth which supposes that an already existing divine-human being descends from heaven, divesting himself of some of his prerogatives, undergoing humiliations, and finally ascending to his former position of honour. This is a sample of space imagery (just as the Day of Christ is time imagery)—it was not intended literally and should not be interpreted literally. When used in a hymn to Christ, it expresses our response to the one who was both humiliated and exalted, in terms of the reality that lies beyond human existence.

That last sentence provides plenty of material for theological questions and answers, without confusing the issue by a mythical picture that no longer corresponds to our real ways of thinking. The Christological hymn is still a supremely important starting point for thought about Christ, provided we realize that it is a hymn and not the description of a journey from heaven to earth and back.

A NOTE ON BOOKS

F. W. Beare's *Commentary on the Epistle to the Philippians* (Black's New Testament Commentaries, 1959) gives a good list of books and is itself a valuable contribution to the study of Philippians. R. P. Martin's commentary on and introduction to *The Epistle of Paul to the Philippians* (Tyndale New Testament Commentaries, 1959) is a more conservative, verse-by-verse interpretation. Between them, these two books exhibit the divergent opinions which have been mentioned earlier. Help in understanding Pauline ideas in Philippians and their background may be obtained from C. K. Barrett's book *From First Adam to Last* (Black, 1962).

✶   ✶   ✶   ✶   ✶   ✶   ✶   ✶   ✶   ✶   ✶   ✶   ✶

THE FIRST AND SECOND LETTERS OF PAUL TO THE THESSALONIANS

PAUL IN MACEDONIA AND ACHAIA

THE FIRST AND SECOND LETTERS OF PAUL TO THE

THESSALONIANS

✻　✻　✻　✻　✻　✻　✻　✻　✻　✻　✻　✻　✻

THE THESSALONIAN CHURCH

In the course of a first journey to Greece, and probably in
A.D. 49, Paul arrived at Thessalonica from Philippi where he
had received 'injury and outrage' (1 Thess. 2: 2). He was
accompanied by Silvanus and Timothy and, despite the activity of opponents, they proclaimed the gospel fearlessly and
made converts from the Gentile population (1 Thess. 1: 9). He
taught them—or at least expected them to understand—a
great many of the fundamental Christian convictions about
God as Father, Jesus Christ as Lord (especially the significance
of his death and resurrection and his expected coming as
deliverer), and the work of the Holy Spirit in the Church.
There was a ready hearing for his teaching about the near approach of the Day of the Lord—that is the final day when
justice would be handed out, wrongs would be righted, and
those who were worthy would share God's 'kingdom and
glory' (1 Thess. 2: 12). He taught them the connexion of
faith, love and hope; passed on 'the tradition of the way we
must live to please God' (1 Thess. 4: 1); did his best to show
them a life of integrity and good sense by working for his
own support (though he also received help from the church
at Philippi, Phil. 4: 16); and persuaded them that a Christian
Church, in fellowship with the Lord Jesus Christ, has been
chosen by God, not to exist for itself alone, but to lead the
Gentiles to salvation (1 Thess. 2: 16).

This information from 1 Thessalonians corresponds well

enough with the account in Acts 17: 1–4, but corrects the impression that Paul spent there only three or four weeks. A considerably longer period is implied by the pastoral relation established between Paul and the converts, and by the repeated help sent from Philippi. The account in Acts continues with a lively narrative about the Jewish instigation of a riot, the intervention of the magistrates, and Paul's hurried departure for Beroea. When he resumed preaching in this new centre and had some success, the Thessalonian Jews tried the same tactics. As a result, Paul was provided with an escort to Athens, while Silvanus and Timothy stayed behind.

Despite these misfortunes for Paul, the church at Thessalonica made rapid and encouraging progress. Its members became 'a model for all believers in Macedonia and Achaia. From Thessalonica the word of the Lord rang out; and not in Macedonia and Achaia alone' (1 Thess. 1: 7–8). Even if this contains some courteous exaggeration, Paul's words make it plain that the church had established its reputation. No doubt this was due in part to the city's importance. It stood on the busy main road, the Via Egnatia (from the Adriatic to the eastern part of the empire), at its junction with another main road northwards to the Danube. It was a free state enjoying great prosperity; it was the capital of the province of Macedonia, its most populous city, and its largest port.

The church's progress was soon complicated by external and internal problems. They began to experience the hostility of their fellow-countrymen; they had to suffer hardship and stand up for their faith (1 Thess. 2: 14; 3: 2). Among their own number, some became faint-hearted, others behaved irresponsibly (1 Thess. 5: 14). Some among them died and the church was thrown into great perplexity. An intense longing for Jesus' return excited but did not comfort them. They had their 'leaders and counsellors' (1 Thess. 5: 12), it is true, but these were not distinct from or set over the congregation; and their founder and apostle was far away in Athens.

But they were constantly in his prayers (1 Thess. 1: 2, 3)

and he was 'exceedingly anxious to see' them again. Plans to visit Thessalonica came to nothing, so Paul sent Timothy to encourage them and bring back news (1 Thess. 2: 17 — 3: 5). It is clear that, at some point, Silvanus and Timothy had rejoined Paul, probably at Athens. From Acts it is not possible to obtain a clear picture of their movements, and it does not much matter. When Timothy returned (Acts 18: 5 suggests that Paul had by then moved on to Corinth), he brought news that the Thessalonians were standing firm but were also in need of help with their various problems. So Paul wrote the first letter after a fairly short separation from the church (1 Thess. 2: 17), perhaps in A.D. 50.

THE LETTERS

1 Thessalonians has thus a strong claim to be the earliest of the Pauline letters that were preserved. By this time Paul had been a Christian missionary for some fifteen years, and the hand-written conclusion to 2 Thessalonians ('this authenticates all my letters') suggests that earlier ones were written but not preserved. The first half of 1 Thessalonians is so much taken up with the relation of Paul to a particular missionary situation that the letter must owe its preservation to the special instruction given in 4: 13 — 5: 11 about Christians who had died and the coming of Jesus. But the same facts demonstrate that this is a genuine letter, and not a disguised pamphlet or early Christian forgery to propagate views about Christ's return. The absence of teaching about the Mosaic Law, justification by faith, and other themes dominant in Galatians and Romans simply means that controversy on the matters was not yet central and played no part in Thessalonian church life. If the style or language of the letter is compared with that of other Pauline letters, the evidence (though not all on one side) does nothing to upset these general conclusions.

The second letter is not different in style from the first, but it has features which make its genuineness open to question.

It is sent by the same three writers, and the only place where they are known to have been together is Corinth (according to the evidence of Acts). Presumably then the second letter, like the first, was written during Paul's period of eighteen months in that city. The situation at Thessalonica is much the same. Though the hardships of the Thessalonians now included actual persecution (2 Thess. 1: 4), the irresponsible elements in the church needed much firmer handling (2 Thess. 3: 6–16), and false announcements that the Day of the Lord had already come demanded a repetition of teaching about events that must first take place (2 Thess. 2: 1–12). It has sometimes been suggested that the relation of the two letters can more easily be understood if 2 Thessalonians was in fact sent before 1 Thessalonians (e.g. the remark in 1 Thess. 5: 1, that 'about dates and times, my friends, we need not write to you', is meaningful if they already know the programme of events described in 2 Thess. 2: 1–12). But the personal explanations of 1 Thess. 2: 17 — 3: 10 are convincing evidence that 1 Thessalonians was Paul's first written communication with the church after he left them; and what he says in 2 Thessalonians fits a situation that was getting out of hand more rapidly than he expected in 1 Thessalonians. It has often been remarked that his tone is more formal and less approving in the second letter. This is scarcely surprising. In 1 Thessalonians he has to answer their perplexed questionings about the Christian dead. They wonder whether they have displeased God and forfeited their expectation of being with Christ at his coming. In 2 Thessalonians he has to explain why Christians are 'bound to thank God' (2 Thess. 2: 13) despite hardship, death, and a delayed expectation of Christ's arrival as deliverer. If he speaks somewhat more formally, it is to give force and authority to his assurances.

Even if a reasonably satisfactory account can be given of circumstances in Thessalonica that called for 2 Thessalonians in reply, the main difficulty has not yet been dealt with. Many readers find the instruction in 2 Thess. 2: 1–12 objectionable in itself, without parallel in Paul's other writings, and in contradiction with 1 Thessalonians. For the first letter says that the Day of the Lord comes suddenly, like a thief in the night (1 Thess. 5: 1-3), whereas the second describes (or seems to describe) a series of events by which the coming will be recognizable. Those who regard this argument as a disproof of Paul's authorship suggest that 2 Thessalonians was written towards the end of the first century by a follower of Paul who wished to explain why Christ had not come (at least in an open and observable manner) though Paul had taught that his coming was near. The letter illustrates one way of dealing with an important problem in the early Church. It had to abandon its temporary plans for a brief interval before Christ's return, and to make new ones for an indefinite period of history—hence the instructions for moderating religious excitement and for settling down to some honest work.

This is an impressive objection, if indeed the early Church was forced to make a great reappraisal of its way of life when the Lord's return was indefinitely postponed; but the evidence for this new alignment is not persuasive. Nor is the contradiction between the teaching of the two letters well founded. In 2 Thess. 2: 1-10 Paul uses highly pictorial, symbolic language side by side with language drawn from ethical teaching to describe the same 'final rebellion against God'. He does not necessarily intend the symbolic language to be taken literally, but expects it to be interpreted by the kind of language we use when we talk of the choice between right and wrong. What he says in both letters means that the Day of the Lord will come at a time determined entirely by God in a situation when men are shutting their eyes to the truth. This is the point of both 1 Thess. 5: 3-6 and 2 Thess. 2: 10-12.

'While they are talking of peace and security, all at once calamity is upon them, sudden as the pangs that come upon a woman with child; and there will be no escape. But you, my friends, are not in the dark, that the day should over-take you like a thief. You are all children of light, children of day. We do not belong to night or darkness, and we must not sleep like the rest, but keep awake and sober.'

'Destroyed they shall be, because they did not open their minds to love of the truth, so as to find salvation. There-fore God puts them under a delusion, which works upon them to believe the lie, so that they may all be brought to judgement, all who do not believe the truth but make sin-fulness their deliberate choice.'

Christians recognize this situation and are ready at any time, for when God finally intervenes, he will act suddenly. Even if the language of the two letters is not fully consistent, any Jewish teacher would have felt at home with an approach that required some conflict of ideas to express the fullness of the truth.

The objections to Pauline authorship are not compelling, and, granted our fragmentary knowledge of the situation at Thessalonica, a reasonable account can be given of the second letter as part of Paul's dealings with a young, Gentile Christian church. It has sometimes been thought surprising that a second letter, on very much the same themes, should have been required within so short a time. Apart from proposals to regard 2 Thessalonians as really addressed to another church (for which the evidence is lacking), it has been suggested that Paul intended it for a Jewish-Christian minority at Thessalo-nica, but there is no evidence that the letter was addressed to a minority or that the Christian community was divided in this way. There is rather more to be said for the suggestion that Paul was specially thinking of the church leaders when writing the second letter, but it is clear that the leaders were not a group distinct from the whole congregation.

THE CONTENTS OF THE LETTERS

1 THESSALONIANS

CHAPTER 1

CHAPTER 2

CHAPTER 3

CHAPTER 4

CHAPTER 5

✻   ✻   ✻   ✻   ✻   ✻   ✻   ✻   ✻   ✻   ✻   ✻   ✻

THE FIRST LETTER OF PAUL TO
THE THESSALONIANS

Hope and Discipline

FROM PAUL, Silvanus, and Timothy to the congrega- **1**
tion of Thessalonians who belong to God the Father
and the Lord Jesus Christ.

Grace to you and peace.

✴ The ancient custom of beginning a letter by naming the
writer and the intended readers is here used with greater
simplicity than in other Pauline letters, except 2 Thessalonians. Without comment, Silvanus and Timothy are joined
with Paul as people already known. Presumably, therefore,
Silvanus is the same person as the Silas who accompanied Paul
in establishing a Christian community at Thessalonica, according to Acts 17: 1–9. Timothy is not mentioned at this
precise point in Acts, but chapter 16: 1–5 tells how Paul made
him a member of his company when he set out on the journey
that later took him to Thessalonica: and the statement of
Acts 17: 14 that 'Silas and Timothy both stayed behind'
when Paul went south from Beroea suggests that Timothy
was with Paul and Silas shortly beforehand at Thessalonica.
When this letter was being written, he had just returned to
Athens from a visit to Thessalonica (1 Thess. 3: 2, 6).

The word *congregation* with which the readers are addressed,
translates the very common Greek word *ekklesia*, which meant
a properly summoned assembly of the citizens (as in Acts
19: 39: 'it will be dealt with in the statutory assembly'), but
was not used of a religious gathering. In the Septuagint, the
Greek translation of the Old Testament, it had been used to

translate a Hebrew word meaning the gathering of Israel as God's people; and for this reason was adopted by the early Christians to describe their own local gatherings. On the same model, they often distinguished their use of the word from the non-religious meaning by adding a qualifying phrase, e.g. 'the congregations in Judaea, God's people in Christ Jesus', 1 Thess. 2: 14; 'the congregations of God's people', 2 Thess. 1: 4.

In the greeting of both letters, the qualifying phrase *who belong to God* etc. is somewhat unusual; literally it reads 'in God...and the Lord Jesus Christ'. Paul occasionally follows the example of the Greek Old Testament (e.g. Ps. 60: 12, 'In God we shall do valiantly', which clearly means 'by God's help') and speaks of doing something in God, as he does at 1 Thess. 2: 2, but he does not elsewhere speak of a group of people as being in God. He seems to be using a familiar Greek idiom meaning in the power of, or belonging to, God—thus distinguishing the *ekklesia* he is writing to from the regular assembly of Thessalonian citizens. He adds 'in the Lord Jesus Christ', which is a very familiar and distinctive Pauline expression. It is capable of a great variety of applications, many of them implying a corporate experience of belonging to Christ (e.g. 'by our fellowship with the Lord Jesus' in 1 Thess. 4: 1 represents 'in the Lord Jesus').

The word *Lord* might describe anyone with authority over others, e.g. the owner of a group of slaves; but it also had a familiar religious meaning to Paul's readers, since it was used as a title for the gods of popular cults and, in the Greek Old Testament, appeared instead of the sacred name of the Jewish deity. Paul uses it of Christ very frequently in these two letters; what, as a Jew, he had learnt to say of God he now also applies to Christ—except that the Lord Jesus Christ had suffered as men suffer and would return as judge and saviour. Consequently, he is the bringer of God's *grace* and *peace*. Both these words, in other letters, give rise to important teaching about reconciliation; here, however, they belong to the fixed language of worship and are not developed further. ✶

A SHARED EXPERIENCE

We always thank God for you all, and mention you in 2
our prayers continually. We call to mind, before our God 3
and Father, how your faith has shown itself in action,
your love in labour, and your hope of our Lord Jesus
Christ in fortitude. We are certain, brothers beloved by 4
God, that he has chosen you and that when we brought 5
you the Gospel, we brought it not in mere words but in
the power of the Holy Spirit, and with strong conviction,
as you know well. That is the kind of men we were at
Thessalonica, and it was for your sake.

And you, in your turn, followed the example set by us 6
and by the Lord; the welcome you gave the message
meant grave suffering for you, yet you rejoiced in the
Holy Spirit; thus you have become a model for all be- 7
lievers in Macedonia and in Achaia. From Thessalonica 8
the word of the Lord rang out; and not in Macedonia and
Achaia alone, but everywhere your faith in God has
reached men's ears. No words of our are needed, for they 9
themselves spread the news of our visit to you and its
effect: how you turned from idols, to be servants of the
living and true God, and to wait expectantly for the 10
appearance from heaven of his Son Jesus, whom he raised
from the dead, Jesus our deliverer from the terrors of
judgement to come.

✻ Paul follows a pattern fairly common in ordinary Greek
letters, and continues with a thanksgiving to God. This provides him with a natural introduction to his first purpose in
writing the letter, namely a desire to encourage Christians at
Thessalonica in their hardships. He expresses gratitude, it is

true, for the quality of their faith, but goes further and includes even their suffering in his thanksgiving. This is possible because the apostle and the Church are bound closely together by experiences they have shared, not only when Christianity was first proclaimed in the city but also in later events.

3. This carefully phrased sentence brings together *faith*, *love*, and *hope* to represent the full Christian life. (There is a similar intention in the more pictorial words of 5:8, 'armed with faith and love for breastplate, and the hope of salvation for helmet'; and, in the familiar words of I Cor. 13:13, Paul says that 'there are three things that last for ever: faith, hope, and love; but the greatest of them all is love'.) The three words indicate allegiance to 'the living and true God', expressed in acts of self-forgetting goodness, and leading to an ultimate confidence that Christ's work, now begun, will be completed. Interwoven with these thoughts are the words *action*, *labour* (i.e. heavy work), and *fortitude* or endurance, in an increasing scale of severity, to emphasize that life in the Church cannot be dissociated from activity and hardship.

4-5. The suggestion of hardship is now offset by the conviction that God has loved and chosen the Thessalonian converts, and by the evidence of the effectiveness of the Gospel in themselves as well as in the apostle and his fellow missionaries. (It is possible to translate slightly differently and to take the effectiveness of the Gospel as proof that they had been chosen: *We are certain...that he has chosen you* because *when we brought you the gospel, we brought it not in mere words...*; but the meaning is not greatly changed.) Many centuries earlier, especially at the times of the Exodus and the Exile, the Israelites had been strengthened by the conviction that they were God's loved and chosen people. This privilege carried with it the responsibility to obey God and demonstrate his love: 'the Lord set his heart in love upon your fathers and chose their descendants after them, you above all peoples... You shall therefore love the Lord your God, and keep his charge, his statutes, his ordinances, and his commandments

62

always' (R.S.V. Deut. 10: 15 — 11: 1). The prophet of the
Exile explicitly taught that they had been chosen to serve
God: 'You are my witnesses, says the Lord, and my servant
whom I have chosen, that you may know and believe me and
understand that I am He' (Isa. 43: 10). This teaching was
transferred by Paul from the Jewish people to the new, mainly
Gentile, Christian communities. Since he mentions it without
further explanation, both here and in the second letter ('from
the beginning of time God chose you to find salvation in the
Spirit that consecrates you, and in the truth that you believe',
2 Thess. 2: 13), it must presumably have formed part of his
initial explanation of *the Gospel*.

It was also closely related to the description *brothers* which is
particularly frequent in these two letters. In Jewish religion,
members of God's chosen people were regarded as brothers
in a great family; in the New Testament, the term is still
applied to Jews but in most places has become the standard
name for fellow-Christians. It marks the continuity between
the old people of God and the new; whereas the quality which
distinguishes the new community is *the power of the Holy
Spirit*. Not that this power was unknown to the Jews, though
it was generally confined to special people at particular times.
Some hoped that the day would come when God would give
the Spirit as the common and constant possession of all the
people (Joel 2: 28), and the first Christians believed that among
them this hope had been fulfilled (and indeed Peter said so
on the day of Pentecost, Acts 2: 16–18). Paul takes for granted
that God indeed bestows the Holy Spirit on his readers (4: 8),
that they saw this power demonstrated when the Gospel was
preached to them, and now experience it themselves when
they can rejoice even in grave suffering (1: 6).

6. One consolation in their suffering is that they were not
alone; others had experienced it: Paul himself quite recently
(2: 2) and earlier the Lord Jesus. In 2: 14 they are reminded
that they 'have fared like the congregations in Judaea'. The
literal translation would be 'have become imitators of the

congregations'; but the N.E.B. translation properly represents the meaning, and it would have been possible to do something similar in the present passage: 'you shared the experience that we had, and the Lord too'. The idea of conscious imitation is perhaps not directly suggested.

7–9. The vigorous and steadfast faith of the church had set the pattern for all Christians in *Macedonia and in Achaia* (the northern and southern provinces that constituted Greece); and even beyond, their record was known apart from any commendation by Paul.

9–10. The encouragements so far given are now strengthened by a reminder of what was said and done when they first became Christians; and these verses provide important information about Paul's way of presenting 'the Gospel' to Greeks. The approach is thoroughly Jewish. When he says that they had *turned from idols* (a word used in the Greek Old Testament to stress the illusory character of heathen deities) *to be servants of the living and true God*, he echoes the scorn of the prophets: 'Their idols are like scarecrows in a cucumber field, and they cannot speak; they have to be carried for they cannot walk. Be not afraid of them, for they cannot do evil, neither is it in them to do good... But the Lord is the true God; he is the living God and the everlasting King. At his wrath the earth quakes, and the nations cannot endure his indignation' (R.S.V. Jer. 10: 5, 10).

In verse 10 *the terrors of judgement to come* might more literally be translated 'the approaching wrath'. It is precisely God's ability to show active hostility against wickedness and evil that makes him *living and true*. It must be understood, however, that 'wrath' is being used in a rather special manner. In the early days of the Greeks and the Romans, as well as of the Hebrew people, it was commonplace to regard bad luck and sudden disaster as divine punishment, or even as the irrational wrath of the gods. The god was pictured behaving emotionally like an angry and powerful king, though the writers of the Old Testament were seldom in danger of mistaking this symbolic language for literal statement. Later more reflective writers hesitated to speak of God's anger at all, and Paul shared their reluctance. Of eighteen passages in his letters where the word is used, only three explicitly speak of 'the wrath of God'; others refer to 'wrath' (N.E.B. 'the terrors of judgement', 5: 9) or 'the wrath' (N.E.B. 'retribution', 2: 16), as if this were something not exactly impersonal—since no relation of God to man can be impersonal—but somewhat remote from God. Despite these qualifications, and the tension that was sometimes felt between God's wrath and his love, the old symbolic word seems to have been retained to express the conviction that God does not remain unmoved by wickedness and evil. He responds warmly to the wrongs done by his people and the wrongs done to them by others. In part his wrath was thought to be at work in the happenings of human life and historical events (which may be the meaning of 'retribution' in 2: 16), but its full effect was reserved for the final reckoning. At the last day, the wrath would be let loose upon Gentiles and faithless Jews alike, and the world would enter upon a period of suffering from which even the faithful would not escape untouched.

A Christian form of this Jewish expectation is elaborated in 2 Thess. 1: 6–10, and there are other references to it at the end of the first letter. It seems to have been introduced here to suggest that Christian hardships are a first experience of the expected period of suffering. Christians are not exempt; yet they have a *deliverer* from the approaching wrath. This too is a Jewish thought, arising by reflection on the sacrifice of the Jewish martyrs in the struggle against oppression during the years 175–141 B.C. In an account of the conflict, a Jewish patriot about to die speaks to his torturers: 'I, like my brothers, give up body and life for the law of our fathers, appealing to God to show mercy soon to our nation and by afflictions and plagues to make you confess that he alone is God, and through me and my brothers to bring to an end the wrath of the Almighty which has justly fallen on our whole nation'

(2 Macc. 7: 37–38 R.S.V.; the background of this conflict is described on pages 28–31 of *Understanding the New Testament*, in this series). That the suffering of one man, especially an innocent one, might effect the deliverance of his people was a powerful idea in Judaism, and it provided the clue by which the first Christians recognized what the death of Jesus had accomplished.

The distinctively new feature in this statement of familiar Jewish themes by Christian preachers was the central position of Jesus: his death, resurrection, departure to heaven, and expected appearance again. This was the central core of the apostolic preaching, as is shown by a brief reference in Acts 17: 2–3 to Paul's message in the synagogue at Thessalonica: 'he argued with them, quoting texts of scripture which he expounded and applied to show that the Messiah had to suffer and rise from the dead. "And this Jesus," he said, "whom I am proclaiming to you, is the Messiah."' Jews would understand the significance of this demonstration: the Messiah (a Hebrew word meaning 'anointed', and referring to the practice of appointing kings and others by the ritual use of oil) was God's appointed restorer and leader of his people, foreshadowed in scripture and long expected. But Gentile listeners, lacking the Jewish tradition, would scarcely grasp this meaning; and although the word Christ (the Greek translation of Messiah) was freely used in the hellenistic Church, it was usually as a second personal name of Jesus, not a title or description. The most favoured title of Jesus was Lord, as in the phrase 'our Lord Jesus Christ'; the most important description is *Son* of God. Doubtless this can be regarded as Jesus' self-description, though less from direct statements about himself than from his special way of referring to God as his Father; but it came alive when the earliest Christians began to reflect about Jesus and explain his death and resurrection from scripture. In preaching at Pisidian Antioch, Paul said: 'We are here to give you the good news that God, who made the promise to the fathers, has fulfilled it for the children by raising

Jesus from the dead, as indeed it stands written in the second
Psalm: "You are my son: this day have I begotten you"' (Acts
13: 32–33). It is hard to find evidence that the Jews called
the Messiah the Son of God; but the description was well
established in the hellenistic world for persons possessing
divine powers, and it therefore offered a possibility of con-
veying to Gentiles what Jewish Christians had learnt to see
in Jesus.

When Christians are said *to wait expectantly for the appearance
from heaven of his Son Jesus*, Paul characteristically expresses
the sense of an impending great event, to be marked by the
presence of Jesus who fully represents the will and intention
of God. In the Thessalonian letters, *heaven* is mentioned only
as the place from which Jesus will come ('the Lord himself will
descend from heaven', 4: 16; 'when our Lord Jesus Christ is
revealed from heaven', 2 Thess. 1: 7). When people try to
make a picture of their relation to God, *heaven* is the place
where God lives, earth where men dwell. But Jewish writers
often go further and use *heaven* as another way of speaking
about God himself. To say that *his Son Jesus* will come *from
heaven* implies that he will come with the full power of God. ✳

APOSTOLIC HARDSHIPS

You know for yourselves, brothers, that our visit to you   **2**
was not fruitless. Far from it; after all the injury and out-   2
rage which to your knowledge we had suffered at Philippi,
we declared the gospel of God to you frankly and fearlessly, by the help of our God. A hard struggle it was.
Indeed, the appeal we make never springs from error or   3
base motive; there is no attempt to deceive; but God has   4
approved us as fit to be entrusted with the Gospel and
on those terms we speak. We do not curry favour with
men; we seek only the favour of God, who is continually

5 testing our hearts. Our words have never been flattering
words, as you have cause to know; nor, as God is our
6 witness, have they ever been a cloak for greed. We have
never sought honour from men, from you or from
anyone else, although as Christ's own envoys we might
7 have made our weight felt; but we were as gentle with
8 you as a nurse caring fondly for her children. With
such yearning love we chose to impart to you not only
the gospel of God but our very selves, so dear had you
9 become to us. Remember, brothers, how we toiled and
drudged. We worked for a living night and day, rather
than be a burden to anyone, while we proclaimed before
you the good news of God.

10   We call you to witness, yes and God himself, how devout and just and blameless was our behaviour towards
11 you who are believers. As you well know, we dealt with
you one by one, as a father deals with his children, appealing to you by encouragement, as well as by solemn
12 injunctions, to live lives worthy of the God who calls
you into his kingdom and glory.

* Attention is now given to certain particular hardships which
Paul and his companions had undergone. At Philippi, before
reaching Thessalonica, Paul and Silas had been accused of
creating a public disturbance and advocating un-Roman
practices; and the magistrates, not realising that they were
Roman citizens, had yielded to the clamour of the mob, and
had flogged and imprisoned them (Acts 16: 19–38). On
arrival at Thessalonica, their bold preaching had meant *a hard
struggle*, presumably against Jewish opposition (Acts 17: 5). It
may be that memory of Jewish accusations, and even knowledge that they were being renewed in his absence, cause Paul
at this point to defend himself with obvious feeling. He, as

well as his Gospel, could be hurt by misunderstanding and misrepresentation.

The charges that could be levelled against his teaching can be discerned by noting what he repudiated. If he felt it necessary to justify himself, no doubt he also wished to arm his readers with good arguments against opponents. In reply, he appeals to his sense of responsibility to God, his pastoral concern for the converts, and his actual practice and teaching.

3. Elsewhere *error* is translated 'delusion' (2 Thess. 2: 11), and *base motive* in 4: 7 is translated 'impurity'. Together with *deceive*, and the suggestions of flattery and greed in verse 5, they are somewhat emotional words and consequently difficult to define and answer. They sketch in the reputation of the travelling religious charlatan, well known in the ancient world, with whom Paul contrasts himself.

4. In contrast, Paul is strongly aware that it is not he but God who decides what is taught (it is 'the gospel' or 'good news of God' in verses 2, 8 and 9) and who should teach it. It is God who helps them to declare it (verse 2) and whose *favour* rewards them, just as it is *God who is continually testing our hearts* (i.e. our real motives) and stands by his servants to support them in their cause ('God is our witness', verses 5 and 10). It is God who calls men and provides the standard of a worthy life (verse 12).

6. The conviction that 'God has approved us as fit to be entrusted with the Gospel' is summed up in the word *envoys*, which translates the Greek *apostoloi* (Eng. 'apostles'). This was almost entirely a Christian word to describe a group, not confined to the Twelve, of missionary leaders in the earliest days of the Church who had received a special commission to be witnesses of the risen Christ and to be his representatives.

9. Paul's statement that *he worked for a living* tells his readers that he knows from experience what their own labour had meant (1: 3), disposes of any suggestion that he had made money out of his converts, and prepares the ground for dealing with a group of people in the church who are

unwilling to provide for themselves (4: 11-12; this last problem is dealt with more fully in 2 Thess. 3: 6-12). It is not surprising that a Jewish teacher should earn his living as a craftsman, for the rabbis approved of independence (the collection of Jewish teachings from the early centuries A.D., called the Jerusalem Talmud, says: 'Hire yourself out to work that is beneath your dignity rather than become dependent on others') and laid it down that 'a man is obliged to teach his son a trade, and whoever does not teach his son a trade teaches him to become a robber'. According to Acts, Paul was a tentmaker by trade (18:3) and at Ephesus claimed to have earned enough for himself and his companions (20: 34). References in the Corinthian letters show how much he desired 'the satisfaction of preaching the Gospel without expense to anyone' (1 Cor. 9: 18); but this seems to mean that he would not take money from the people among whom he was working, though he accepted support from previously established churches. When thanking the Philippians for a later gift he remembered that 'even at Thessalonica you contributed to my needs, not once but twice over' (Phil. 4: 16, and there is similar information in 2 Cor. 11: 7-9).

12. This verse expresses one of the deepest motives in the ethical teaching of the New Testament: that conduct should be suited to the nature of the God whom men worship. The same appeal is made in 2 Thess. 1: 5. References to the kingdom or sovereignty of God are infrequent in Paul's writings and most of them are the basis of ethical appeals. In accordance with Old Testament language of worship, God is portrayed as a king whose greatness is shown by his glory or splendour, and whose subjects are expected to offer appropriate obedience. The dominant theme in the teaching of Jesus was that God's kingdom had drawn near and was available to needy and penitent people. The influence of Jesus on Paul's thinking can be traced in his statement that God calls men to participate in his *kingdom and glory*. ✳

THE CHURCH'S HARDSHIPS

This is why we thank God continually, because when we 13
handed on God's message, you received it, not as the
word of men, but as what it truly is, the very word of
God at work in you who hold the faith. You have fared 14
like the congregations in Judaea, God's people in Christ
Jesus. You have been treated by your countrymen as
they are treated by the Jews, who killed the Lord Jesus 15
and the prophets and drove us out, the Jews who are
heedless of God's will and enemies of their fellow-men,
hindering us from speaking to the Gentiles to lead them 16
to salvation. All this time they have been making up the
full measure of their guilt, and now retribution has overtaken them for good and all.

✶ Paul repeats the thanksgiving of 1: 2 and immediately
mentions the hardships undergone by the Thessalonian
church, as if to suggest the spirit in which Christians should
accept the consequences of their faith; but with this he com-
bines the thought of God's judgement on those who cause
the hardships.

13. Paul strongly asserts that the message transmitted by
human preachers was rightly received as spoken by God. In
force and authority it was therefore similar to prophetic
speech. Consequently it was a most grave fault to reject it or
hinder its spread; but those *who hold the faith* experience *the
very word of God at work in* them; that is, *God's message* spreads
by their agency to the neighbouring areas (1: 8) and the same
message is effective in their own life. (This explanation is un-
necessary if the phrase is translated, somewhat less probably,
by *the very word of God* who is *at work in you*.)

15–16. This sudden attack on *the Jews* is surprising. Jewish
opposition at Thessalonica may have been at the root of the

church's hardships, though Paul blames only 'your country-men'. When he speaks of *the Jews* elsewhere they are almost always contrasted with the Gentiles, and are never merely the opponents of the Christians (as they so frequently are in John's Gospel). The verdict that *now retribution has overtaken them for good and all* is in strong contrast with his view in Rom. 9 — 11 ('God has not rejected the people which he acknowledged of old as his own', 11: 2; 'this partial blindness has come upon Israel only until the Gentiles have been admitted in full strength; when that has happened, the whole of Israel will be saved', 11: 25–26). To say that the Jews were *enemies of their fellow-men* echoes the common misunderstanding and suspicion of them in the ancient world, and is unexpected on the lips of a devout Jew.

This last observation may contain a clue to understanding Paul's reason for writing these verses, unless we adopt the rather desperate suggestion (for which other evidence is lacking) that they were not written by Paul but were added by a later hand. The very strangeness of a Jew speaking like a Gentile about his own people suggests that the price he had paid for becoming a Christian was growing separation from the people of his own race and religion. He may wish his Gentile readers to understand that such alienation is one of the hardships to be expected; if they had been excluded from the society of their fellow countrymen, he and other Jewish Christians had experienced the same. So of course had the *Lord Jesus* in the first place, and even before his coming the Jews had killed God's earlier messengers, the prophets. The A.V. reads 'their own' *prophets* in agreement with a large number of later Greek manuscripts and with the anti-Jewish, heretical writer Marcion in the second century. The word 'own' was presumably added to exclude the possibility that prophets, since they are mentioned after the Lord Jesus, meant Christian prophets. The word-order is no more than a way of writing, and means: they *killed the Lord Jesus* as well as *the prophets*. Jewish cruelty to the prophets was stressed by Jesus

('O Jerusalem, Jerusalem, the city that murders the prophets and stones the messengers sent to her!' Matt. 23: 37) and was taken up by Stephen in his defence before the Jewish Council: 'Was there ever a prophet whom your fathers did not persecute? They killed those who foretold the coming of the Righteous One; and now you have betrayed him and murdered him' (Acts 7: 52).

Such a reading of Jewish history was accepted only by those who took a special view of God's will for his people which they believed the Jews had persistently rejected. According to Paul, God willed the *salvation* of the Gentiles, and his own calling as an apostle depended on this conviction: 'In his good pleasure God, who had set me apart from birth and called me through his grace, chose to reveal his Son to me and through me, in order that I might proclaim him among the Gentiles' (Gal. 1: 15–16). The word *salvation* is itself a characteristically Jewish description of all that God offers to faithful and obedient people.

It implies that they are rescued from enemies and from the consequences of their own wrong choices, and given a share in God's security and strength. In the Old Testament the most profound exploration of these ideas in their consequences for groups of people and individuals is contained in Isa. 40—55, and it is notable that salvation extends beyond the Jews. God, speaking to his servant the prophet as representative of the whole people, says, 'It is too light a thing that you should be my servant to raise up the tribes of Jacob and to restore the preserved of Israel; I will give you as a light to the nations, that my salvation may reach to the end of the earth' (Isa. 49: 6). In Paul's teaching, *salvation* is strongly 'eschatological': that means, it is part of God's final judgement on mankind, so that 'the full attainment of salvation' can be contrasted with 'the terrors of judgement' (5: 9). More positively, being saved means to 'possess for your own the splendour of our Lord Jesus Christ'; and though that still lies in the future, there is a present experience of 'salvation in the spirit that

73

consecrates you, and in the truth that you believe' (2 Thess. 2: 13–14).

This train of thought is brought to an end with two prover-bial expressions. One, *the full measure of their guilt*, is as old as Gen. 15: 16 and arises from the conception that God allows the nations a good deal of freedom but sets a limit to the amount of wrong they can do. This manner of speaking was used by Jesus when he said to the scribes and Pharisees 'You are the sons of those who murdered the prophets. Fill up then the measure of your fathers'; and the words are to be under-stood metaphorically, not literally, as the N.E.B. translation shows: 'Go on then, finish off what your fathers began' (Matt. 23: 31–32). Paul's intention is best illustrated by 2 Macc. 6: 14–15 R.S.V.: 'In the case of the other nations the Lord waits patiently to punish them until they have reached the full measure of ther sins; but he does not deal in this way with us, in order that he may not take vengeance on us afterward when our sins have reached their height.' In Paul's view, Jewish opposition to the salvation of the Gentiles has reached the limit, *and now retribution has overtaken them for good and all.*

Almost exactly these words appear as a kind of proverbial ending to a brief account of the vengeance on Shechem (the story is told at length in Gen. 34) in the popular Jewish writing called the *Testaments of the Twelve Patriarchs* (*Test. Levi* 6: 11). The significance of this fact, however, is not clear since discoveries in the Qumran caves make it possible that the form of the Testament of Levi which contains these words may be Jewish-Christian. As Paul uses them here, there are problems of translation (since the Greek rendered *for good and all* may equally well mean 'at last') and of inter-pretation. If Paul intended something more precise than a forceful expression of God's displeasure (*retribution* is literally 'wrath') there are three possibilities. (1) He may be referring to a recent disaster, such as the death of twenty thousand Jews when Cumanus was Roman procurator in Judaea (A.D. 48–52), according to a report by the Jewish historian

Josephus (*Jewish Antiquities*, xx. 5, 3). It has usually been thought, however, that an event of more international consequence would be needed to suggest to Gentiles at Thessalonica that retribution had really overtaken the Jews. Such an event would be the capture and destruction of Jerusalem by the Romans in A.D. 70 at the end of the Jewish revolt; in which case it would have to be supposed that at least the end of verse 16 was added to the letter at a later time. (2) If this solution is rejected, Paul may mean that the obstinate attitude of the Jews has settled their fate. They will not accept Jesus, and they try to prevent others from accepting him. Therefore he will not be their 'deliverer from the terrors of judgement to come' (1: 10). Since the judgement then seemed so near at hand, Paul spoke with prophetic certainty in forecasting God's final verdict on the Jews. If this view is correct, then Paul must have thought again before he wrote Romans. The quotations from Rom. 11 already given at the beginning of this note show his conviction that God had not abandoned the Jews after all. (3) It is possible, however, to reconcile what he says here with his view in Rom. 9 — 11 if he meant to say, not that the final fate of the Jews was now settled, but that God's appointment of the Jewish people to be his servant to enlighten the Gentiles was now cancelled. According to his teaching in Rom. 1: 18, 24, 26, and 28, one way in which the divine retribution falls on wicked men is that God gives them up to the wickedness they persist in choosing. Since they refuse to serve him by leading the Gentiles to salvation, he refuses to have them any longer as his servants. ✷

THROUGH HARDSHIP TO JOY

My friends, when for a short spell you were lost to us— 17
lost to sight, not to our hearts—we were exceedingly
anxious to see you again. So we did propose to come to 18
Thessalonica—I, Paul, more than once—but Satan

19 thwarted us. For after all, what hope or joy or crown of pride is there for us, what indeed but you, when we stand

20 before our Lord Jesus at his coming? It is you who are indeed our glory and our joy.

3   So when we could bear it no longer, we decided to

2 remain alone at Athens, and sent Timothy, our brother and God's fellow-worker in the service of the gospel of

3 Christ, to encourage you to stand firm for the faith and, under all these hardships, not to be shaken; for you know

4 that this is our appointed lot. When we were with you we warned you that we were bound to suffer hardship; and

5 so it has turned out, as you know. And thus it was that when I could bear it no longer, I sent to find out about your faith, fearing that the tempter might have tempted you and my labour might be lost.

6   But now Timothy has just arrived from Thessalonica, bringing good news of your faith and love. He tells us that you always think kindly of us, and are as anxious to

7 see us as we are to see you. And so in all our difficulties

8 and hardships your faith reassures us about you. It is the breath of life to us that you stand firm in the Lord.

9 What thanks can we return to God for you? What thanks for all the joy you have brought us, making us

10 rejoice before our God while we pray most earnestly night and day to be allowed to see you again and to mend your faith where it falls short?

* Paul now turns to his highly personal concern for the Thessalonian Christians, making plain that their fortunes are reflected in his own emotions. He wishes to encourage them *under all these hardships, not to be shaken* (or, 'beguiled away' as it may possibly be translated); and the good news of their

continuing *faith and love* gives him a present joy that anticipates
the future rejoicing when men *stand before our Lord Jesus at
his coming*. He therefore repeats and rounds off the thanksgiving with which the letter began.

18. The Hebrew word *Satan* means first an opponent, and
then someone who accuses, whether truly or falsely. Occasionally in the Old Testament, more frequently in the New,
the figure of Satan appears as a source of inexplicable evil.
He obstructs good intentions (Paul may mean that he himself was ill or that his plans went astray) and uses any kind of
hardship to undermine faith. Hence he is called 'the tempter'
(3: 5) since, if he has no cause to accuse people, he sets out
to obtain one. Whether he brings his accusations before the
divine court and to that extent acknowledges God, or constantly tries to overthrow the divine order (as he seems to do
in 2 Thess. 2: 9), is never quite clear. Nor need it be, since
it was not Paul's intention to provide information about
demonic beings but to speak forcibly about evil without
suggesting that it can finally escape God's control.

19–20. It is characteristic that Paul's expectation at the
coming of the Lord Jesus is bound up with what happens to
his fellow-Christians, just as now 'it is the breath of life to us
that you stand firm in the Lord' (3: 8). This sense of inter-
dependence in the Christian life appears again in the eschatological imagery of the letters, as at 3: 13 and 4: 15–18.

3: 2. It is also present in the words *God's fellow-worker*,
which may be understood to mean Paul's 'fellow-worker for
God'. Only 1 Cor. 3: 9 has a similar phrase; it is possible that
here Paul simply wrote (what is found in one early manuscript) 'our brother and fellow-worker', and that ancient
copyists remembered the Corinthian passage and made this
one the same.

3: 10. With candid words about the limitations of their
faith, Paul makes room for the instructions in the second half
of the letter. ✶

LITURGICAL CLOSE

11 May our God and Father himself, and our Lord Jesus,
12 bring us direct to you; and may the Lord make your
love mount and overflow towards one another and to-
13 wards all, as our love does towards you. May he make
your hearts firm, so that you may stand before our God
and Father holy and faultless when our Lord Jesus comes
with all those who are his own.

⁂ The first, thanksgiving part of the letter is brought to a
close with a paragraph in the style of worship. The thought
of God's judgement which will take place *when our Lord Jesus
comes*, introduces the two subjects next discussed.

13. At first sight the words *all those who are his own* suggest a
return of Jesus accompanied by faithful Christians. Presumably they are those who have died before his coming, and
the future of such Christians is indeed the subject of 4: 13–14.
The Greek words could more literally be translated 'with all
his holy ones' (or 'saints', as in R.V., R.S.V.), and it is Paul's
constant practice to use this expression for members of the
Christian Church. A similar phrase in 2 Thess. 1: 10 refers to
'the presence of the Lord..., when on that great Day he
comes to be glorified among his own and adored among all
believers'; but this pictures a return of Jesus not with but to
his faithful people. A little earlier, in 2 Thess. 1: 7, the 'Lord
Jesus Christ is revealed from heaven with his mighty angels';
and so it is possible that 'holy ones' are to be understood in a
common Old Testament sense as angels. There is no doubt
that Paul is using a phrase from Zech. 14: 5: 'Then the Lord
your God will come, and all his holy ones with him' (R.S.V.).
It expresses the splendour and finality of the Lord's return
and, since it is liturgical language, perhaps ought not to be
examined further. ⁂

INSTRUCTIONS ON CONDUCT

And now, my friends, we have one thing to beg and **4**
pray of you, by our fellowship with the Lord Jesus. We
passed on to you the tradition of the way we must live to
please God; you are indeed already following it, but we
beg you to do so yet more thoroughly.

For you know what orders we gave you, in the name 2
of the Lord Jesus. This is the will of God, that you should 3
be holy: you must abstain from fornication; each one of 4
you must learn to gain mastery over his body, to hallow
and honour it, not giving way to lust like the pagans who 5
are ignorant of God; and no man must do his brother 6
wrong in this matter, or invade his rights, because, as we
told you before with all emphasis, the Lord punishes all
such offences. For God called us to holiness, not to im- 7
purity. Anyone therefore who flouts these rules is 8
flouting, not man, but God who bestows upon you his
Holy Spirit.

About love for our brotherhood you need no words of 9
mine, for you are yourselves taught by God to love one
another, and you are in fact practising this rule of love 10
towards all your fellow-Christians throughout Macedonia. Yet we appeal to you, brothers, to do better still.
Let it be your ambition to keep calm and look after your 11
own business, and to work with your hands, as we 12
ordered you, so that you may command the respect of
those outside your own number, and at the same time may
never be in want.

✳ When a Christian community was created by the preaching
of the gospel, the converts were taught how to behave as well

as what to believe. They received not only 'God's message' (2: 13) but also *the tradition of the way we must live to please God* (that is, to gain approval as his servants). This kind of tradition is referred to again in 2 Thess. 2: 15 and 3: 6 in order to deal with a particular problem of conduct. Perhaps for a similar reason, Paul here reinforces the principles of holiness and love within the Christian community. These principles were *orders* which had been given them *in the name of the Lord Jesus* (that is, on his authority). Since the readers had been taught *the tradition*, it is not set out in full but only mentioned; hence, what was plain to them is not always clear to us.

2–8. The N.E.B. translation gives a plain meaning: *you* (the Christian community) *must abstain from fornication*. This requires *each one of you . . . to gain mastery over his* [own] *body*; and also, as far as others are concerned, not to *do his brother wrong in this matter*. In the demand for purity, there is a responsibility to yourself and to others.

This is perhaps the best meaning that can be got out of the Greek, but it is by no means certain, since several words have more than one possible interpretation. The word *matter* can also mean 'lawsuit', and even 'business dealings'. This would give the sense 'no man must overreach his brother in his business' (or 'in lawsuits'); but the whole passage is about holiness and purity, and there is no reason to suppose that the subject changes in the middle. Much more difficult are the words *gain mastery over his body*, for Paul is in fact less explicit. The word here translated *body* is translated 'pot' in 2 Cor. 4: 7: 'We are no better than pots of earthenware to contain this treasure'; and it means any kind of jar or instrument. Since the comparison of the human body to a jar, containing (it may be) the soul, was common in Greek writers, this metaphorical use would not be novel to the Thessalonians. Yet there is nothing in the context (as there is in 2 Cor. 4) to enlighten the readers, and it may be that Paul had already taught them that the human body is, as it were, a jar containing the Holy Spirit (see verse 8, and compare 1 Cor. 6: 19: 'Your body is a shrine of the indwelling Holy Spirit').

A different interpretation of the jar metaphor appears in R.S.V. (though not the Catholic Edition): 'to take a wife for himself'. This has the merit of giving the Greek verb its common meaning 'to acquire' (the evidence that it could mean *gain mastery over* is not strong), and of making good sense throughout the passage. But there is no good reason for supposing that Paul's readers would understand the metaphor in this way, and there is no trace of it in his teaching elsewhere.

It is worth noting that the passage contains three Old Testament reminiscences which are infrequent elsewhere in this letter. *The pagans who are ignorant of God* (verse 5) is from Jer 10: 25 and Ps. 79: 6, and refers to their worship of many gods and their disobedience of the one God's moral demands. *The Lord punishes* (verse 6) echoes such passages as Ps. 94: 1; and *bestows upon you his Holy Spirit* (verse 8) is reminiscent of Ezek. 36: 27 and 37: 14. This suggests that Paul's teaching about holiness to Gentile converts relied considerably on the Jewish moral tradition which associated polytheism with unfaithfulness in both senses, the religious and the sexual. The kind of teaching given can be seen clearly in Rom. 1: 18–32.

Holy, *hallow* and *holiness* were originally ritual words, applied to whatever had been separated from common use and appropriated for God's service. Without ever losing the ritual meaning, the scope of the words was extended and their meaning modified in two ways: (1) the quality of holiness was not confined to certain special people, but was to be the property of the whole people of God; and (2) since the imperfect and defiled were excluded from God's service, his people must be pure both morally and ritually. The way is open for God's people to become holy by their obedience to his will, but it is God himself who can make them 'holy in every part' (5: 23); it is the Holy 'Spirit that consecrates' them (2 Thess. 2: 13).

11–12. Fuller information in 2 Thess. 3: 6–12 about the condition of the church suggests that a lively expectation of Christ's return had unduly excited some Christians. They had given up their regular work and were 'minding everybody's business but their own'. They were likely to give the church a bad name and to require support from church funds. Hence these instructions.

The New Testament provides plenty of evidence that they were needed more than once in the early days of the Church. Christians no doubt learnt such sayings of Jesus as these from the Sermon on the Mount: 'Do not store up for yourselves treasure on earth, where it grows rusty and moth-eaten'; and 'I bid you put away anxious thoughts about food and drink to keep you alive' (Matt. 6: 19, 25). Some responded with impulsive enthusiasm, especially when they thought that Jesus would soon return, and surrendered their possessions and their jobs. The Christians at Jerusalem, for example, 'held everything in common; they would sell their property and possessions and make a general distribution as the need of each required' (Acts 2: 45). But before long they were asking Paul to 'keep their poor in mind' (Gal. 2: 10) and he had to organize a programme of inter-church aid to help them: 'Macedonia and Achaia have resolved to raise a common fund for the benefit of the poor among God's people at Jerusalem' (Rom. 15: 26, and compare 1 Cor. 16: 1–3; 2 Cor. 8–9). In other words, careful planning and forethought had to supplement enthusiastic devotion and repair its mistakes. Paul's instructions to the Thessalonians show how Christians began to think out their responsibility for work and possessions, not to contradict the words of Jesus but in order to carry out what they implied in their own situation. Compare the words of 1 Tim. 5: 8: 'If anyone does not make provision for his relations, and especially for members of his own household, he has denied the faith and is worse than an unbeliever.' ✻

UNTIL THE LORD COMES

We want you not to remain in ignorance, brothers, 13 about those who sleep in death; you should not grieve like the rest of men, who have no hope. We believe that Jesus 14 died and rose again; and so it will be for those who died as Christians; God will bring them to life with Jesus.

For this we tell you as the Lord's word: we who are 15 left alive until the Lord comes shall not forestall those who have died; because at the word of command, at the 16 sound of the archangel's voice and God's trumpet-call, the Lord himself will descend from heaven; first the Christian dead will rise, then we who are left alive shall 17 join them, caught up in clouds to meet the Lord in the air. Thus we shall always be with the Lord. Console one 18 another, then, with these words.

About dates and times, my friends, we need not write 5 to you, for you know perfectly well that the Day of the 2 Lord comes like a thief in the night. While they are 3 talking of peace and security, all at once calamity is upon them, sudden as the pangs that come upon a woman with child; and there will be no escape. But you, my friends, 4 are not in the dark, that the day should overtake you like a thief. You are all children of light, children of day. We 5 do not belong to night or darkness, and we must not 6 sleep like the rest, but keep awake and sober. Sleepers 7 sleep at night, and drunkards are drunk at night, but we, 8 who belong to daylight, must keep sober, armed with faith and love for breastplate, and the hope of salvation for helmet. For God has not destined us to the terrors 9 of judgement, but to the full attainment of salvation

10 through our Lord Jesus Christ. He died for us so that we, awake or asleep, might live in company with him.
11 Therefore hearten one another, fortify one another—as indeed you do.

✳ The transition from the unsettling effect of anticipating Christ's return to the anxieties associated with it is not unnatural; but some special circumstance seems to have called for the developed treatment that now follows. It falls into two paragraphs, 4: 13–18, and 5: 1–11, which are closely linked. Both end with similar encouragements: *We shall always be with the Lord. Console one another* (17–18), and we shall *live in company with him. Therefore hearten one another* (10–11), the Greek words for *console* and *hearten* being identical. Both paragraphs contrast *the rest* (*of men*) (4: 13 and 5: 6) with Christians, and both use *sleep* as a metaphor for death; though the second paragraph also uses *sleep* to mean spiritual insensitivity. Both refer to one of the central themes of early Christian preaching, the death and resurrection of Jesus, in order to draw conclusions about the survival of Christians with Him (4: 14 and 5: 10). And finally, the same imagery is present in both. In the first, the Lord descends to begin the final battle against evil and Christians go to meet him; in the second, they are wearing their armour, ready for his arrival. It seems likely, therefore, that the two paragraphs are dealing with the same question, not different ones.

What that question is can best be discovered from verse 15: *we who are left alive until the Lord comes shall not forestall those who have died.* It can be inferred that certain Christians had died, leaving the church in sorrow and perplexity. Why had this *calamity* come upon them? Had they, in distinction from Christians who remained alive, displeased God? Would they therefore forfeit their expectation of being with Christ at his return?

Paul answers these questions along the following lines: (1) Christians who have died are in no worse case than those who are still alive. (2) Proper arrangements have been made for the Christian dead when Christ returns. (3) In any case, Christians alive or dead belong to the new age of light and will not be lost in darkness. (4) The real peril is not to *sleep in death*, but to be spiritually insensitive and complacent.

There are parallels to some of this teaching in the Fourth Gospel, as when Jesus says, 'I am the light of the world. No follower of mine shall wander in the dark; he shall have the light of life' (John 8: 12); and also, 'In very truth I tell you, you will weep and mourn, but the world will be glad. But though you will be plunged in grief, your grief will be turned to joy. A woman in labour is in pain because her time has come; but when the child is born she forgets the anguish in her joy that a man has been born into the world. So it is with you, for the moment you are sad at heart; but I shall see you again, and then you will be joyful, and no one shall rob you of your joy' (John 16: 20–22).

The teaching in the Fourth Gospel on this theme makes little use of the traditional imagery of Jewish writing about the last days, and Paul also can manage without it. But in the Thessalonian letters he uses it freely. There are notable parallels to his language in the War Rule of the Qumran community. This contains instructions for a final conflict to take place between the devout Jews of Qumran and their enemies, and may have been composed at the end of the first century B.C. or the beginning of the first century A.D. This document describes itself as 'the Rule of War on the unleashing of the attack of the sons of light against the company of the sons of darkness'. Before the discovery of the Dead Sea Scrolls, the obviously Hebraic expression *sons of light* was unknown outside the New Testament. The War Rule says that 'for the sons of darkness there shall be no escape. The seasons of righteousness shall shine over all the ends of the earth; they shall go on shining until all the seasons of darkness are consumed, and at the season appointed by God, his exalted greatness shall shine eternally'. This is parallel to Paul's statements in 5: 1, 3; and the general similarity is strengthened by a reference to 'a time of great tribulation for the people which God shall redeem'. These quotations are taken from the War Rule I (in G. Vermes, *The Dead Sea Scrolls in English*, p. 124); column III lists the various trumpets that sound the battle calls, and column XVII refers to the help given by 'the might of the princely angel of the kingdom of Michael'. Compare *the archangel's voice and God's trumpet-call* in 4: 16.

No doubt the men of Qumran understood the War Scroll literally, but such language can be symbolic. It can be read as a confident use of battle imagery to express the conviction that God would really fight victoriously for his people. This was certainly the Christian method. It is not suggested that Paul borrowed ideas and images from the scroll, but simply that he used a Jewish convention of his day with equal freedom and with more spiritual intentions. In these two paragraphs we have to discover the serious meaning of symbolic language. For an attempt to do so, see the comment below on verses 15–17 and the final section on The Significance of the Letters.

13. The use of *sleep* as a metaphor for death, is common in Jewish and Greek life; it cannot be pressed to give information about the condition in which the dead exist. The *hope* which *the rest of men* lack is not the expectation of surviving death, though for many death was indeed the end; but, as other references to the word show, the confidence that Christians would be with Christ at his return.

14. In the Greek the final words are simply *God will bring them with Jesus* which seems to mean that they will return 'in company with Jesus'. But this does not exactly follow from the belief that *Jesus died and rose again*, and in verse 16 the first result of the Lord's descent is the resurrection of 'the Christian dead'. Hence the N.E.B. interpretation: *God will bring them to life with Jesus*.

15–17. Paul's own reply to the Thessalonians' problem is given in verse 15. It is justified by the statements of verses

86

16–17. *As the Lord's word.* This may mean that they are otherwise unrecorded sayings of Jesus, though he cannot have
uttered them in their present form since *the Lord himself,
the Christian dead,* and *we who are left alive* are written from the
viewpoint of the early Church. Otherwise they may have been
a disclosure in vision or prayer, of the same kind that led
Paul in I Cor. 15: 51 to say, 'Listen! I will unfold a mystery:
we shall not all die, but we shall all be changed in a flash...at
the last trumpet-call'. In both letters Paul naturally writes as
if he himself would be among the living when Christ returned, though in Phil. 1: 20–26 his thoughts turn to the
possibility of his own death.

For Greek readers, two semi-technical words would make
the scene immediately clear. In the words *until the Lord
comes,* Paul uses the official term for a royal visit to the provinces, corresponding to which is the formal procession that
goes out *to meet* the approaching emperor. This familiar hellenistic occasion is filled out with Jewish apocalyptic imagery,
much of which is derived from the encounter between God,
Moses and the people at Sinai in Exod. 19: 10–17. There also
the Lord is said to *descend from heaven* on the mountain, sur-
rounded by thick *clouds,* the *trumpet-call* was sounded, and
Moses led the people out of the camp *to meet the Lord.* Paul
adds the sound of the archangel's voice from traditional
Jewish story-telling, and *the word of command* to represent the
divine emperor giving the signal for his troops to advance.
At Sinai, however, when the people go *to meet the Lord* they
are halted at the foot of the mountain and only Moses is
allowed to ascend. But at the coming of Christ no Christian,
whether living or dead, is prevented from reaching up to
the descending Jesus.

This imagery is acceptable if we take it for what it was
intended to be, not a programme of events, but an assertion of
faith. It means (1) that God will come to us in all his might;
(2) that, as once he acted to create a people for himself at
Sinai, so he will now act to create his final people; (3) that no

one who has learnt to serve him through Christ need be excluded; and (4) that the outcome will be a life raised above these present hardships and griefs, for *we shall always be with the Lord*.

5: 2. *The Day of the Lord* is an Old Testament expression of the popular hope that one day God would fight on behalf of his people and give them final victory over the enemy nations. In the teaching of the prophets, Israel was warned that God would fight against his own people as well as the nations: his victory would be the execution of divine judgement on all wickedness. In similar vein, Paul adapts a parable of Jesus ('if the householder had known what time the burglar was coming he would not have let his house be broken into', Luke 12: 39) to represent the Day as a threat to the unwary.

5: 3. Similar teaching is recorded in Luke 21: 34–36: 'Keep a watch on yourselves; do not let your minds be dulled by dissipation and drunkenness and worldly cares so that the great Day closes upon you suddenly like a trap; for that day will come on all men, wherever they are, the whole world over. Be on the alert, praying at all times for strength to pass safely through all these imminent troubles and to stand in the presence of the Son of Man.'

5: 4–8. In a very similar passage in Rom. 13: 11–14, Paul says: 'It is far on in the night; day is near. Let us therefore throw off the deeds of darkness and put on our armour as soldiers of the light.' When Jesus returns, darkness will be replaced by the full light of day. But the metaphor is also used rather flexibly with a moral meaning. *Darkness*, *sleep*, and being *drunk* are symbols of an insensitive and complacent attitude, whereas Christians should be properly enlightened people. The picture of the soldier, much more elaborately drawn in Eph. 6: 13–17, comes from Isa. 59: 17 where God himself goes forth to battle having 'put on righteousness as a breastplate, and a helmet of salvation upon his head'. The prophet meant that he was certain of the justice of God's cause (the meaning of righteousness in this context) and his final victory (which is how *salvation* should be translated in Thessalonians also). According to Paul, the Christian too is confident of victory, and relies as well not only on the justice of his cause but on faith and love.

5: 9. The word *destined* expresses an important theme in Paul's thinking, which appears again in 2 Thess. 2: 13: 'from the beginning of time God chose you to find salvation in the Spirit'. But this can easily be made to mean more than he intended. Far from asserting that God has decreed for each man an inescapable destiny, Paul wishes to deny that God has irrevocably destined some for the terrors of judgement (which the Thessalonians feared might be true of the Christians who had died). God is on our side and always has been, even though hardship 'is our appointed lot' (3: 3). The encouragement in 2: 12 'to live lives worthy of God who calls you into his kingdom and glory' suggests that men must claim what God has reserved for them.

5: 10. *Awake or asleep* now means alive or dead; the original metaphor of 4: 13 is resumed. ✳

VARIOUS INSTRUCTIONS

We beg you, brothers, to acknowledge those who are 12 working so hard among you, and in the Lord's fellowship are your leaders and counsellors. Hold them in the 13 highest possible esteem and affection for the work they do.

You must live at peace among yourselves. And we 14 would urge you, brothers, to admonish the careless, encourage the faint-hearted, support the weak, and to be very patient with them all.

See to it that no one pays back wrong for wrong, but 15 always aim at doing the best you can for each other and for all men.

16, 17, 18   Be always joyful; pray continually; give thanks whatever happens; for this is what God in Christ wills for you.

19, 20   Do not stifle inspiration, and do not despise prophetic
21   utterances, but bring them all to the test and then keep
22   what is good in them and avoid the bad of whatever kind.

* Paul urges the church to support its leaders, to promote harmony and discipline, and to give a discerning welcome to religious enthusiasm.

12. It is difficult to imagine any Christian group without its *leaders*; but our earliest evidence, which is all in Paul's letters, points to something less formal than an official order of ministers. It is true that Acts 14: 23 (which was written later than Thessalonians though it refers to an earlier stage of Paul's life) says that Barnabas and Paul 'appointed elders for them in each congregation'; though in fact Paul never uses the word 'elder' until the Pastoral Letters (which may not be by Paul). It looks as if Paul at first supervised the churches by his own authority as an apostle, and expected each congregation to follow the custom of Jewish life and to respect those who established themselves as local leaders by their hard work and wise counsel. He first mentions more formal names of church officers when he refers to the 'bishops and deacons' at Philippi (Phil. 1: 1).

14. *Admonish the careless* would be, in more modern language, 'remind the irresponsible of their duties'. A hint of irresponsible behaviour has already been given in 4: 11, and the matter is fully dealt with in 2 Thess. 3: 6–12.

15. The principle that a Christian retaliates by doing good was deeply felt in the early Church. Paul again refers to it in Rom. 12: 17–21; it is taught in 1 Pet. 3: 9 and reflects the teaching of Jesus himself, Matt. 5: 38–48.

16. Paul has already mentioned that the Thessalonians 'rejoiced in the Holy Spirit' when they became Christians (1: 6), and has referred to the joy they gave him by their

steady faith (2: 19–20; 3: 9). This is very similar to the theme of rejoicing that runs through Philippians (see the introductory note to Phil. 1: 3–11). In Gal. 5: 22 ('the harvest of the Spirit is love, joy, peace...') he makes it plain that joy is to be expected as a natural result of experiencing the liberating power of God. In 2 Thessalonians, though he tells his readers why they should thank God, despite their hardships, he does not actually refer to joy again.

17–18. It was one of Paul's most deeply felt convictions that the Christian life should be constantly allied to prayer. 'Persist in prayer' (Rom. 12: 12). 'Persevere in prayer' (Col. 4: 2). 'Give yourselves wholly to prayer and entreaty; pray on every occasion in the power of the Spirit' (Eph. 6: 18). He himself practised what he preached. 'We always thank God for you all, and mention you in our prayers continually' (1 Thess. 1: 2). Naturally this included praying to God for the benefit of others, and he expected others to pray for him (verse 25). But it is a notable feature of his intercessions that they are often linked with thanksgiving, as here. The same is true of requests for oneself in Phil. 4: 6: 'in everything make your requests known to God in prayer and petition with thanksgiving.' The prayer that asks for something is joined with the prayer that acknowledges what has already been received.

19–20. Worship in Gentile Christian churches was lively and sometimes eccentric. What Paul means by *inspiration* and *prophetic utterances* can be seen in 1 Cor. 14. Such spontaneous enthusiasm comes from the pressure of the Spirit on the Church's life, and is not to be stifled; yet it could be misguided and misleading. The 'oracular utterance' mentioned in 2 Thess. 2: 2 is an example.

21. As it stands, this verse advises the readers to distinguish the good from the bad in prophetic utterances; but the Greek could have a more general meaning. The N.E.B. footnote puts a full stop after *utterances*, and then translates: 'Put everything to the test; keep hold of what is good and avoid every kind of evil.' *

CONCLUDING LITURGY

23 May God himself, the God of peace, make you holy in every part, and keep you sound in spirit, soul, and body,

24 without fault when our Lord Jesus Christ comes. He who calls you is to be trusted; he will do it.

25   Brothers, pray for us also.

26   Greet all our brothers with the kiss of peace.

27   I adjure you by the Lord to have this letter read to the whole brotherhood.

28   The grace of our Lord Jesus Christ be with you!

✳ 23. *Spirit, soul and body* is a rhetorical phrase, of the same kind as 'you shall love the Lord your God with all your heart, and with all your soul, and with all your might' (Deut. 6: 5). It means 'your whole being', and no conclusions can be drawn from it about Paul's view of human nature. For an explanation of Christ's coming, see the comments on 1: 10; 2: 19–20; 3: 13; and 4: 15–17.

26. *The kiss of peace* mentioned also at the end of the Roman and Corinthian letters (and in a different form in 1 Pet.) was an informal and natural gesture of family solidarity. Later it became a part of the liturgy under the name adopted by the N.E.B. translation. Paul actually wrote 'holy [or ritual] kiss'.

27. Strictly, to *adjure* people to do something means to invoke God's punishment on them if they fail. Even if Paul is speaking (presumably to the leaders, who may have been specially in mind since verse 14) in popular style, this demand that the letter should be read to all is very strong. It has been suggested that he is thinking of some tension between the leaders and the church, or some division between Jewish and Gentile Christians; but his previous lavish praise of the church scarcely supports this. It may be his intention to stress the formal character of the letter as an apostolic communication,

somewhat as he authenticates 2 Thessalonians by adding his signature. Whatever the reason, this command is an important step in the formation of Christian worship and in the process by which Paul's letters became part of scripture. ✲

✲   ✲   ✲   ✲   ✲   ✲   ✲   ✲   ✲   ✲   ✲   ✲   ✲

THE SECOND LETTER OF PAUL TO
THE THESSALONIANS

Hope and Discipline

GREETING

1 F ROM PAUL, Silvanus, and Timothy to the congregation of Thessalonians who belong to God our Father and the Lord Jesus Christ.
2 Grace to you and peace from God the Father and the Lord Jesus Christ.

⁎ A slightly expanded form of the opening of 1 Thessalonians. ⁎

THE JUSTICE OF GOD'S JUDGEMENT

3 Our thanks are always due to God for you, brothers. It is right that we should thank him, because your faith increases mightily, and the love you have, each for all and 4 all for each, grows ever greater. Indeed we boast about you ourselves among the congregations of God's people, because your faith remains so steadfast under all your 5 persecutions, and all the troubles you endure. See how this brings out the justice of God's judgement. It will prove you worthy of the kingdom of God, for which indeed you are suffering.

6 It is surely just that God should balance the account by 7 sending trouble to those who trouble you, and relief to you who are troubled, and to us as well, when our Lord Jesus Christ is revealed from heaven with his mighty

angels in blazing fire. Then he will do justice upon those 8
who refuse to acknowledge God and upon those who will
not obey the gospel of our Lord Jesus. They will suffer 9
the punishment of eternal ruin, cut off from the presence
of the Lord and the splendour of his might, when on that 10
great Day he comes to be glorified among his own and
adored among all believers; for you did indeed believe
the testimony we brought you.

With this in mind we pray for you always, that our 11
God may count you worthy of his calling, and mightily
bring to fulfilment every good purpose and every act
inspired by faith, so that the name of our Lord Jesus may 12
be glorified in you, and you in him, according to the
grace of our God and the Lord Jesus Christ.

* This part of the letter comprises an expanded thanksgiving
(which in the Greek is one long, loosely connected sentence,
verses 3–10) and a prayer for the Church. We should understand its meaning better if we knew the situation in Thessalonica for which it was written. As it is, we can only make
conjectures. It is therefore worth noting that the thanksgiving
is repeated at 2: 13 with similar added emphasis ('we are
bound to thank God for you') as if Paul felt called on to
justify his insistent gratitude. Further, he begins by praising
the Thessalonians' *faith*, *love* and even endurance (verses 3–4)
but says nothing about hope until 2: 16. It would fit such
facts as we have if we supposed that their hope, weakened by
persecutions and *troubles*, needed strengthening. In the first
letter it has already been necessary to 'encourage the faint-
hearted' (1 Thess. 5: 14).

It is possible to imagine the church leaders hard put to
answer the questions that arose. How could Paul so confidently
give thanks for a church in trouble? Why should *believers* be
persecuted, while *those who refuse to acknowledge God* go

95

unchecked? Why was the Lord so long in coming to the rescue of *his own*? Paul therefore reminds them of the features in their present situation that call for thanksgiving (1: 3–4), shows them the justice of God's forthcoming judgement (1: 5–10), and then offers an explanation of the delayed return of Jesus (2: 1–12).

5. Paul takes for granted what he had asserted in 1 Thessalonians: that 'God calls you into his kingdom' (1 Thess. 2: 12) and that 'we are bound to suffer hardship' (1 Thess. 3: 4). But it is not at once clear *how this brings out the justice of God's judgement*. Perhaps the train of thought can be drawn out in the following way: 'Your endurance of persecution has in fact strengthened your faith and love and will therefore fit you for the kingdom of God. Since you know that God's judgement will be just, present trouble is an indication that your recompense is certain.' Or Paul may be referring to the expected period of suffering before the great judgement (it was discussed in reference to 1 Thess. 1: 10), so that their troubles are 'evidence of the righteous judgement of God' (R.S.V.) shortly to take place.

7–10. This rhythmical passage is full of Old Testament phrases and imitations. There is plenty of evidence, including the canticles in Luke 1 and the Hymns of the Qumran Community, that devout Jews practised the art of writing poetry in the style of the Psalms. Paul has used this kind of religious inspiration, not to describe the judgement, but to evoke its majesty and certainty in the minds of his readers. The revelation of Christ *with his mighty angels in blazing fire* recalls God's self-disclosure to Moses when 'the angel of the Lord appeared to him in a flame of fire' (Exod. 3: 2). Association of ideas then suggests 'the Lord will come in fire...to render his anger in fury, and his rebuke with flames of fire' from Isa. 66: 15, and 'pour out thy wrath upon the nations that know thee not, and upon the peoples that call not upon thy name' from R.S.V. Jer. 10: 25. This characteristic piece of poetic parallelism (in which the same thought is repeated in different words) suggests that only one group of people is in mind in verse 8, not two groups such as Gentile persecutors and Jewish instigators. If so, the translation should be: *justice upon those who refuse to acknowledge God and will not obey the gospel.*

The fate of such people is again expressed in words reminiscent of an Old Testament judgement passage: 'Enter into the rock and hide in the dust, from before the terror of the Lord and from the glory of his majesty. The haughty looks of man shall be brought low, and the pride of men shall be humbled; and the Lord alone will be exalted in that day' (Isa. 2: 10–11). But it is notable that here, as earlier, Paul does not limit himself to exact quotation or adopt all the features of this traditional judgement language. He uses it flexibly and makes it serve his conviction that the ultimate disaster (or *eternal ruin*) for mankind is to be *cut off from the presence of the Lord* and denied participation in the *splendour of his might.*

The participation of *mighty angels* in the judgement is a feature derived from Jewish apocalyptic writings which pictured the Lord as an oriental monarch attended and assisted by powerful emissaries. Angels seldom play more than a formal part in Paul's writings, and are not mentioned again in the Thessalonian letters (except perhaps at 1 Thess. 3: 13). At this point he seems to be drawing on the tradition behind such Gospel sayings as: 'All the peoples of the world will make great lamentation, and they will see the Son of Man coming on the clouds of heaven with great power and glory. With a trumpet blast he will send out his angels, and they will gather his chosen from the four winds' (Matt. 24: 30–31). ✳

BEFORE THE DAY OF THE LORD

And now, brothers, about the coming of our Lord Jesus 2
Christ and his gathering of us to himself: I beg you, do 2
not suddenly lose your heads or alarm yourselves,
whether at some oracular utterance, or pronouncement,

or some letter purporting to come from us, alleging that
3 the Day of the Lord is already here. Let no one deceive
you in any way whatever. That day cannot come before
the final rebellion against God, when wickedness will be
revealed in human form, the man doomed to perdition.
4 He is the Enemy. He rises in his pride against every god,
so called, every object of men's worship, and even takes
his seat in the temple of God claiming to be a god himself.
5 You cannot but remember that I told you this while I
6 was still with you; you must now be aware of the
restraining hand which ensures that he shall be revealed
7 only at the proper time. For already the secret power of
wickedness is at work, secret only for the present until the
8 Restrainer disappears from the scene. And then he will be
revealed, that wicked man whom the Lord Jesus will
destroy with the breath of his mouth, and annihilate by
9 the radiance of his coming. But the coming of that wicked
man is the work of Satan. It will be attended by all the
10 powerful signs and miracles of the Lie, and all the decep-
tion that sinfulness can impose on those doomed to
destruction. Destroyed they shall be, because they did not
open their minds to love of the truth, so as to find salva-
11 tion. Therefore God puts them under a delusion, which
12 works upon them to believe the lie, so that they may all
be brought to judgement, all who do not believe the
truth but make sinfulness their deliberate choice.

* Paul's first teaching had led the Thessalonians to expect the
return of the Lord. Following early Christian custom, he seems
to have linked this expectation with the last chapters of Daniel
which were also of interest to many Jewish groups in his day.
Chapters 10–12, in the form of a revelation to Daniel, are

in fact a sketch of Jewish history in the Greek period until the time of Antiochus Epiphanes, who died in 163 B.C. In particular, 11: 29–39 refers in veiled language to his attempted conquest of Egypt which was thwarted by the Romans, his subsequent angry attacks on Jewish institutions and his success in seducing some Jews from their faith. He went so far as to 'exalt himself and magnify himself above every god', but even this horrifying impiety was no hindrance to his remarkable successes.

At this point the apocalyptic writer left the facts as he knew them and turned to prediction (presumably because he was writing at this period of Antiochus' career). In 11: 40–45 he set down the political events by which he expected Antiochus to meet his end. Then follows in 12: 1–3 the arrival of Michael to help the Jews through the worst time of trouble, the deliverance of all who are 'written in the book', and the resurrection of the dead, 'some to everlasting life, and some to shame and everlasting contempt'. It was this story—part history and part symbol—that provided many of the leading features in the Jewish and Christian attempts to discern the future; and it was something based on this that Paul unfolded to the Thessalonians.

It is difficult to imagine what they made of it. To Gentiles, unpractised in Jewish hopes and symbols, it must have been mysterious and puzzling. In the enthusiasm of their newly found faith it gave rise to excitement and uncertainty. Paul's demand, in his first letter, that they should be constantly on the alert because 'the Day of the Lord comes like a thief in the night' (1 Thess. 5: 2) cannot have eased their situation. It is not surprising that some, under the influence of religious emotions, should be gripped by the conviction that *the Day of the Lord is already here.*

Paul therefore returns to teaching already given by word of mouth about the disclosure that must first take place before the Day of the Lord. *That day cannot come before the final rebellion against God.* To describe this rebellion he uses two kinds of language: first symbolic language in verses 3, 4, and 9 about the mysterious figure of evil who does Satan's work; and then moral language in verses 10–12 about the choice between truth and falsehood. This description is twice interrupted. In verses 5–7 he comments on the relation between what has just been said and *the restraining hand*; and then, on resuming the description of the *rebellion* in verse 8, adds an anticipation of the destruction of *that wicked man* by *the Lord Jesus*.

When the description is broken off, Paul has said enough to allay uncertainties in the church, and has said as much as he can to explain the delayed return of Jesus. In the following section he therefore returns to the theme of thanksgiving with which the letter began.

1. *The coming of our Lord Jesus Christ and his gathering of us to himself* are subjects already referred to in 1 Thess. 4: 15–17.

2. The words *purporting to come from us* probably refer to conclusions about the Day of the Lord which some had wrongly made. It is possible that they refer to a letter which was falsely thought to have Paul's authority, and the care he takes to authenticate this letter (3: 17) supports the suggestion. But the instruction at 2: 15 to 'hold fast to the traditions which you have learnt from us by word or by letter' suggests instead that Paul wishes to repudiate, in the strongest terms, a false inference from these traditions.

3, 4, 9. It was commonly believed in the Judaism of Paul's day that a great *rebellion* would take place before God finally came to the rescue of his people. For example, one of the Dead Sea Scrolls is an explanation of the prophecy of Habakkuk in the language of the sect. Interpreting Hab. 1: 5, it says: '"Behold the nations and see, marvel and be astonished; for I accomplish a deed in your days but you will not believe it when told." Interpreted, this concerns those who were unfaithful together with the Liar, in that they did not listen to the word received by the Teacher of Righteousness from the mouth of God...And likewise, this saying is to be interpreted as concerning those who will be unfaithful at the end of the days.' (See G. Vermes, *The Dead Sea Scrolls in English*, p. 233.) Paul, however, is thinking of a general human revolt against God, not merely of unfaithfulness within a religious group.

The commentary is also similar to Paul in its use of 'the Liar', to which there is an obvious parallel in verses 9 and 10. A literal translation brings them even closer, since 'the Liar' represents 'man of lies' in the Hebrew of the Habakkuk commentary, and *wickedness... in human form* (verse 3) is the N.E.B. version of 'man of wickedness' in Paul's Greek. This simply means that the two writings are drawing from the same circle of ideas for different purposes.

THE ENEMY IN JEWISH HISTORY

Paul's symbolic description of the alarming human figure who will challenge all divinity goes back to Daniel's references to Antiochus Epiphanes, helped out by two prophetic descriptions of earlier tyrants, one of Babylon and one of Tyre in Isa. 14: 13–14 and Ezek. 28: 2. Antiochus' most shocking action was to set up a heathen altar in the Temple at Jerusalem. A hundred years later, the Roman general Pompey successfully besieged Jerusalem, and added religious shock to the humiliation of the Jewish defenders by entering the inner Temple. This enormity is referred to in a Pharisaic psalm composed about 50 B.C.: 'When the Sinful Man waxed proud, with a battering ram he cast down fortified walls... Alien nations ascended thine altar, they trampled it proudly with their sandals' (the non-biblical *Psalms of Solomon* 2: 1–2). A hundred years later still, the Temple was again threatened. According to the Jewish historian Josephus (who lived between A.D. 37 and 100), 'the emperor Gaius' accession to power so completely turned his head that he wished to be thought of and addressed as a god... and proceeded to lay sacrilegious hands on Judaea. He ordered Petronius to march with an army to Jerusalem and erect his statues in the Temple:

if the Jews refused them he was to execute the objectors and enslave all the rest of the population' (*The Jewish War*, ii. 10).

In fact the Jews resisted, Petronius played for time, and the emperor died before his order had been carried out; but this happened in A.D. 40, only a decade before the time of this letter. It is not surprising that Paul should still feel the power of the old Antiochus memory to provide a human symbol for the figure behind *the final rebellion*. But whether he ever put a name to this figure or ever thought of him as another imperial tyrant is doubtful. In verse 9 he adds *powerful signs and miracles*, suggesting also the demagogue and religious charlatan, thus drawing on an early Christian tradition which is represented in Mark 13: 22 ('Impostors will come claiming to be messiahs and prophets, and they will produce signs and wonders to mislead God's chosen') and appears in 1 John 2:18 as the Antichrist.

5–7. It is generally thought that *the restraining hand* is some force (or person, *the Restrainer*) which at present prevents the onset of 'the rebellion' and 'the coming of that wicked man'. Paul expects his readers to understand what he means though his language is veiled and his grammar obscure. It is difficult to understand why he describes 'the Enemy' at length, though he told them this while he was still with them, and says nothing to identify *the Restrainer*.

Two types of interpretation have been suggested, the historical and the mythological.

(1) The most ancient and popular suggestion identifies *the restraining hand* with the Roman empire, and *the Restrainer* with the emperor. It appeals for evidence to Paul's approval of 'the existing authorities' in Rom. 13: 1–6; but that same passage is evidence that he did not expect the empire to *disappear from the scene*. It also requires a quick change of mind for the emperor to stand as model for 'that wicked man' at one moment, and to be his restrainer the next. Another suggestion is that the restraining factor is the necessity of

preaching the gospel to all nations (Mark 13: 10) and that *the Restrainer* is Paul himself. But if he had already told them this while he was still with them (and they certainly could not have guessed it from these present words), none of them could suppose that the gospel had now been preached to all nations, nor that 'the Day of the Lord is already here'. Moreover in 1 Thess. 4: 15 Paul assumes that he will be alive when the Day comes, not removed *from the scene.*

(2) The other type of explanation appeals to a widespread ancient myth of the creation which pictures a battle between the Creator and the demon or monster of chaos. The Creator wins, and binds the demon-monster; but the end of creation will be like its beginning—the demon-monster will be unloosed, the battle will be fought again, good will triumph and evil will finally be destroyed. This myth is used in Rev. 20: 1–3: 'Then I saw an angel coming down from heaven with the key of the abyss and a great chain in his hands. He seized the dragon, that serpent of old, the Devil or Satan, and chained him up for a thousand years...After that he must be let loose for a short while.' Perhaps, therefore, Paul wishes to evoke this myth, to suggest that an angel of God is holding back 'the rebellion', 'the coming of that wicked man', and 'the work of Satan'. But to say that the angel then *disappears from the scene* is odd and it does not explain *how already the secret power of wickedness is at work.* Nor is it clear what Paul hoped to achieve by such mystification.

The problem would be different if Paul were still explaining the delay in Christ's coming (not what restrains 'the rebellion'), so that these verses are simply a comment intruded into his description of 'the Enemy'. The following translation and paraphrase gives what might be his meaning: 'You cannot but remember that I told you this while still with you. Well then, you already know what it is that restrains [the Lord's coming], so that he is revealed only at the proper time. For this secret power of wickedness is already at work. He is only the Restrainer until he disappears from the scene, [as in the words] "And then will be revealed that wicked man whom the Lord Jesus will destroy...".'

8. In Hosea God says, 'I have hewn them by the prophets, I have slain them by the words of my mouth, and my judgement goes forth as the light' (Hos. 6: 5). Paul does not mean literal slaughter, but what happens when wickedness and delusion are exposed to the truth.

11–12. Here in germ is Paul's characteristic understanding of the wrath of God (already mentioned in the commentary on 1 Thess. 2: 15–16) by which men are handed over to the consequences of *their deliberate choice*. A fragment of the Dead Sea Scrolls, also concerned with 'the mysteries of sin', suggests his meaning: 'Do not all the peoples loathe iniquity? And yet it is spread by them all. Does not the fame of truth issue from the mouth of all the nations? Yet is there a lip or tongue which holds to it? Which nation likes to be oppressed by another stronger than itself, or likes its wealth to be wickedly seized? And yet which nation has not oppressed another, and where is there a people which has not seized another's wealth?' (See G. Vermes, *The Dead Sea Scrolls in English*, p. 210). ✳

THANKSGIVING AND PRAYER

13 But we are bound to thank God for you, brothers beloved by the Lord, because from the beginning of time God chose you to find salvation in the Spirit that conse-
14 crates you, and in the truth that you believe. It was for this that he called you through the gospel we brought, so that you might possess for your own the splendour of our Lord Jesus Christ.

15   Stand firm, then, brothers, and hold fast to the traditions which you have learned from us by word or by
16 letter. And may our Lord Jesus Christ himself and God

our Father, who has shown us such love, and in his grace
has given us such unfailing encouragement and such
bright hopes, still encourage and fortify you in every good　17
deed and word!

And now, brothers, pray for us, that the word of the　**3**
Lord may have everywhere the swift and glorious
course that it has had among you, and that we may be　2
rescued from wrong-headed and wicked men; for it is
not all who have faith. But the Lord is to be trusted, and　3
he will fortify you and guard you from the evil one.
We feel perfect confidence about you, in the Lord, that　4
you are doing and will continue to do what we order
May the Lord direct your hearts towards God's love and　5
the steadfastness of Christ!

* The emphatic opening thanksgiving is now repeated, on
the ground that Christians, though undergoing persecutions,
are not involved in the ruin of those who have deliberately
chosen 'the Lie'. The Lord will guard them *from the evil
one* and they will possess his splendour for their own.

13. Early manuscript evidence is divided between *aparches*,
which gives the translation *from the beginning...God chose
you*, and *aparchen*, which means 'God chose you as his first-
fruits'. The second is a metaphor drawn from Hebrew sacrificial practice by which the first part of a farmer's produce
was consecrated to God. If this was what Paul wrote, it
implies that the Thessalonian church was only the first
gathering of the Gentile harvest—which may indeed be true,
though it does not obviously spring to mind at this point. The
alternative wording refers God's choice of them (which has
already been discussed in the commentary on 1 Thess. 1: 4–5)
to a decision before history began. There is a similar thought
in Eph. 1: 4: 'In Christ he chose us before the world was
founded.' This kind of statement uses the language of time

to express the conviction that man's destiny for good (and not ultimately for evil) is rooted in the being of God.

The Community Rule of the Qumran sect provides a parallel to Paul's language. 'In the mysteries of His under-standing, and in His glorious wisdom, God has ordained an end for falsehood, and at the time of the visitation He will destroy it for ever...God will then purify every deed of Man with his Truth; He will refine for himself the human frame by rooting out all spirit of falsehood from the bounds of his flesh. He will cleanse him of all wicked deeds with the spirit of holiness' (Community Rule iv. 20–21, see G. Vermes, *The Dead Sea Scrolls in English*, p. 77). Paul, of course, was not writing for an enclosed Jewish group but for an expanding church of Gentile converts, and he attached his assertions to the known 'traditions' about the 'Lord Jesus Christ'.

15–17. After the long explanation in 2: 1–12 which was made necessary by misunderstanding of his earlier teaching (see the comment on 2: 2), Paul now re-affirms *the traditions* which he had taught them *by word or by letter*. He strengthens them to face hardship by reminding them of God's love, grace (which is explained in the note on Phil. 1: 7), and encouragement. He now mentions the *bright hopes* that were notably lacking at the beginning of this letter (see the intro-ductory note on 1: 3–12); and reminds his readers that the Christian life is not merely enduring bravely what must be endured, but a positive activity shown in *every good deed and word*.

3: 1–5. Paul's simple request 'Brothers, pray for us also' in 1 Thess. 5: 25 is here renewed with what is almost a pro-gramme of intercession and petition. They are to pray for the spread of Christian truth, keeping clearly in mind the oppo-sition to it (verses 1–2), but equally remembering God's reliability and power (verse 3). As for themselves, they are to continue in obedience to their apostle and so find *God's love and the steadfastness of Christ* guiding their actions and motives. ✳

CHURCH DISCIPLINE

These are our orders to you, brothers, in the name of our 6
Lord Jesus Christ: hold aloof from every Christian
brother who falls into idle habits, and does not follow
the tradition you received from us. You know yourselves 7
how you ought to copy our example: we were no
idlers among you; we did not accept board and lodging 8
from anyone without paying for it; we toiled and
drudged, we worked for a living night and day, rather
than be a burden to any of you—not because we have not 9
the right to maintenance, but to set an example for you
to imitate. For even during our stay with you we laid 10
down the rule: the man who will not work shall not eat.
We mention this because we hear that some of your 11
number are idling their time away, minding everybody's
business but their own. To all such we give these orders, 12
and we appeal to them in the name of the Lord Jesus
Christ to work quietly for their living.

My friends, never tire of doing right. If anyone dis- 13, 14
obeys our instructions given by letter, mark him well, and
have no dealings with him until he is ashamed of himself. I do not mean treat him as an enemy, but give him 15
friendly advice, as one of the family. May the Lord of 16
peace himself give you peace at all times and in all ways.
The Lord be with you all.

* The tiresome situation dealt with in this section has
already been mentioned in passing at 1 Thess. 4: 11–12 and
5: 14. Presumably, what Paul has now heard (verse 11) means
that the problem is worse. Even when he was with them he
took pains to set them an example and laid down a rule. It

looks as if the church had attracted a few irresponsible people who found it all too easy, in the ferment of excitement about the Lord's coming, to trade on the emotions of others and to live at their expense. Paul deals with them gently but firmly. The church is to hold aloof from a Christian of this kind, to *mark him well, and have no dealings with him until he is ashamed of himself*. This is not expulsion. The church is left to find suitable ways of dissociating itself from such behaviour.

10. The rule means that those who refuse to earn their living do not qualify for church support. *

SIGNATURE

17 The greeting is in my own hand, signed with my name, PAUL; this authenticates all my letters; this is how I
18 write. The grace of our Lord Jesus Christ be with you all.

* This letter was dictated; Paul actually wrote only the final words to give it the authoritative stamp. He claims to be speaking 'in the name of our Lord Jesus Christ' (3: 6), and here takes full responsibility. *

*   *   *   *   *   *   *   *   *   *   *   *   *

THE SIGNIFICANCE OF THE LETTERS

To anyone studying the early history of the Christian Church or interested in the relation of religion and society, the Letters to the Thessalonians are of considerable value. They give information about the origins, hardships, practices and ideas of a group of Christian converts from paganism. The information is not complete and must be supplemented by knowledge of contemporary life, but it is first-hand information from the middle of the first century A.D.

Precisely because it gives an authentic picture of one area of primitive Christianity this information is important for historians and sociologists; but is it important for anyone else? There are two possible reasons for saying that it may be important to everyone: *either* because the ideas it contains and the advice it gives are inherently noble and fruitful, and perhaps even the manner in which they are expressed is beautiful and stimulating; *or* because the Thessalonian Letters are part of the authoritative book of the Christian Church, and describe the source from which our present Christian faith and institutions have developed and the standard by which they should frequently be tested.

Both sorts of answer raise the question how ideas that could be put forward in the first century A.D. can still be meaningful today. It is, of course, true that some ideas may not be affected by time and a change in social conditions; but the Thessalonian Letters contain several that are. Take, as an example, the anxiety of the Thessalonians about Christians who had died. It is true that we find it just as difficult as they did to imagine what happens when someone dies whom we have known very closely. Even the simple conviction that death is the end does not ease that situation. But people who live in the Western world are not constantly worried about death as their forefathers were, and as people in Macedonia certainly were in Paul's day. In great parts of the Western world high birth-rate and high death-rate are no longer our common experience. We have a great deal of knowledge about controlling disease and prolonging life; the chief risks of early, sudden death are of our own making. However much those who are growing old may think about death, the rest are not actively concerned about the problems of a life beyond this one. Consequently they can perhaps understand what the Thessalonians felt, but cannot easily share their feelings.

Christ's Coming

It is even more difficult to share their excited conviction that Christ would soon return and preside at the final judgement. If they really believed that there was very little time left before Christ's visible arrival to distribute rewards and punishments, they were obviously wrong. If further they literally expected a programme of mysterious events to be followed by his descent from heaven, the resurrection of dead Christians, and the flight of other Christians to meet him in the air, they were equally mistaken. Even if they got the time-scale wrong, so that these events are still to happen some thousands of years later, few of us now find it possible to take such imagery literally or to answer the prosaic questions that arise if we do so.

Now, it is well known that teaching about Christ's imminent return has often flourished during the history of the Church, and even today it is a basic principle of faith among some quickly growing Christian groups. Neither in the earliest days of the Church, nor in later times, has the failure of his predicted return destroyed the faith of the believers. This could perhaps mean that people cling to their illusions despite the evidence; but the early Christians, like many later groups, established themselves as a resilient and spreading community in a hostile world. They scarcely give the appearance of a society of people whose main belief had proved false. It is therefore likely that, even in the first place, they were not thinking in purely literal terms of Christ's return but knew (whether they could have expressed it in this way or not) that the language was largely symbolic. To put it in another way, they were using symbols and images as pointers to the truth which might have its fulfilment in Christ's bodily return or in his arrival in some other fashion.

An attempt has been made in the course of the commentary, to suggest how some of these symbols and images can be interpreted. Since to us the imagery is often puzzling and uncongenial, it is natural to ask whether we can now abandon them and retain only the interpretations. This is tempting but unsatisfactory. If the interpretations are clear and precise they will certainly fall short of the full meaning of the imagery; and if they are sufficiently general to express its whole range of meaning they will be unattractive and useless. The great merit of using imagery to talk about convictions and hopes is that it is at once very concrete and very flexible. Once it is realized that imagery is not normally a method of making literal statements, but has to be interpreted with imagination, then the reader himself makes a contribution to what is being read. If the imagery is replaced by reasoned interpretations then the reader has nothing more to do than to accept or reject them.

Underlying Convictions

With this warning in mind, some suggestions can be made about the hopes and convictions that find expression in the imagery of the Thessalonian Letters.

Human existence gains its purpose and its destination from a powerful reality which lies beyond it. It is not a finally meaningless activity, nor does it contain its end in itself.

The final end of human existence is not beyond our knowledge, but has been disclosed to us in Christ. It is disclosed in what we can know of his life and teaching, and it is disclosed in the people who are in communion with him.

The final end of human existence includes a far-reaching judgement about good and evil; and is supported by the conviction that what is good (as judged by the standard of Christ) will ultimately be seen to be good and will persist, whereas what is evil will be seen to be evil and will be destroyed.

This conviction is challenged at every point by powerful forces of evil which seem to make Christ's sacrifice futile and to deny any reality beyond human existence. This contradiction of Christ and God cannot be denied or accounted for; but it is not ultimate or beyond bearing.

There are times when people feel, more or less strongly, that they are moving from one age to another and things will never be the same again. The first converts from Judaism and paganism had this experience and (in a rather different way) we in our own time have experienced the change from the world before to the world after the release of atomic energy and the exploration of space. At some of these turning points of human existence Christ becomes near and his meaning plain. The decisions made at such times are of ultimate significance.

In our personal experience there are occasions when we make decisions of ultimate significance for our own lives. As far as Christians are concerned, these decisions are our response to the presence of Christ. Their effect is not limited to this present life only but to the reality that lies beyond it. Nor is it limited to our own private existence but it extends to the totality of Christ's people, 'living' and 'dead'.

These assertions may sound very different from the imagery that provoked them; anyone else trying to get hold of the underlying convictions would probably state them in other words but equally abstractly. If the reader is dissatisfied, he can try for himself and hope to do better. That is why the imagery is valuable: it is concerned with fundamental convictions about human existence and requires an imaginative response from every reader.

Perhaps it is worth adding a brief comment about Paul's references to Satan or the tempter. There are only three: two are purely conventional, 'Satan thwarted us' (1 Thess. 2: 18) and 'fearing the tempter might have tempted you' (1 Thess. 3: 5); the other is rather more serious, 'the coming of that wicked man is the work of Satan' (2 Thess. 2: 9). On the other hand there are at least fifty references to God, and fifty more to the Lord (Jesus Christ). A study of Paul's other letters shows that he took serious account of contemporary belief in evil forces, even when he scorned them himself; but his experience was overwhelmingly filled, not with Satan, but with God in Christ.

A NOTE ON BOOKS

The leading modern commentaries on the Thessalonian letters are in French and German, but there is a very good one in the Moffatt New Testament Commentary by William Neil, *The Epistles of Paul to the Thessalonians* (Hodder and Stoughton, 1950). More than one mention has been made of G. Vermes, *The Dead Sea Scrolls in English* (Penguin Books, 1962); it provides information about a group within Judaism which shows a number of similarities to primitive Christianity. A survey of the modern study of Paul's teaching, including a chapter on his eschatology, can be found in D. E. H. Whiteley, *The Theology of St. Paul* (Blackwell, 1964).

INDEX

Achaia, 52, 64, 82
Adam, 23, 27
angels, 78, 86, 87, 96, 97, 99, 103
Antichrist, 102
Antiochus Epiphanes, 99, 101
apostle, 69, 73, 90, 92
Asia, 9
Athens, 52, 53, 59
athletics, 26, 30, 46

Babylon, 101
baptism, 29, 39
Barnabas, 90
Barrett, C. K., 48
Beare, F. W., 48
Beroea, 51, 59
bishop, 12, 13, 44, 90
body, 14, 41, 47, 80, 92
book of life, 42
Brundisium, 6
burglar parable, 88
business dealings, 80

Caesarea, 5, 6, 8, 18
Caesar's household, 6, 45
chosen people, 62, 63, 89, 97, 105
church leaders, 13, 32, 56, 90, 92, 95
circumcision, 35–7
citizens, 26
clouds, 87
congregation, 59, 63, 90
Corinth, 10, 53, 54
creation myth, 103
Cumanus, 74

darkness, 85, 88
Day of the Lord, *see* Jesus Christ, Day of Christ
deacons, 12, 13, 44, 90
Dead Sea Scrolls, 12, 85, 86, 96, 100, 104, 106
death of Christians, 54, 84–6, 109

destiny, 62, 63, 89
Divine Redeemer myth, 24, 25, 47
dogs, 35, 36, 40
drunkenness, 88
Dyrrachium, 6

Egypt, 99
elders, 90
'Enemy', 101–103
Epaphroditus, 3, 4, 6, 8, 31
Ephesus, 8–10, 70
episkopos, 12, 13

faith, 38, 51, 52, 62, 71, 77, 95
fear, 29
fire, 96
fornication, 80

Gaius, 101
gnosis, 35, 39, 40
gospel, 14, 15, 30, 51, 62–64, 69, 70, 79, 97, 103
grace, 15, 60, 106

harpagmos, 27
heaven, 67
Heavenly Man, 24
hellenistic, 24
Herod, 18
holiness, 80, 81
Holy Spirit, 18, 37, 51, 63, 73, 81, 90, 91
hope, 51, 62, 86, 95, 99, 106, 111
humility, 26, 47, 97

idols, 64
in Christ Jesus, 12, 26, 46, 47, 60
Israelites, 11, 12, 29, 37, 60

Jerusalem, 10, 73, 75, 101
Jesus Christ
    communion with, 5, 19, 60

114